MW01364804

I AM MY OWN SUPERHERO

Awaken Your Inner Superhero by Igniting
Your Natural Born Superpowers

A STUDENT WORKBOOK ON HOW TO AWAKEN YOUR INNER SUPERHERO THROUGH IDENTIFYING YOUR SUPERPOWERS TO OVERCOME NEGATIVE THINKING, PEER PRESSURE, and BULLYING BY BUILDING SELF ESTEEM, CONFIDENCE, and PERSONAL POWER.

BUILD YOUR OWN SUPERHERO INSIDE THIS WORKBOOK

Award-Winning Fitness Professional

Powered By Erica Humphrey

authorHOUSE®

AuthorHouse™
1663 Liberty Drive
Bloomington, IN 47403
www.authorhouse.com
Phone: 1 (800) 839-8640

Published by AuthorHouse 06/17/2016

ISBN: 978-1-5246-1089-0 (sc)
ISBN: 978-1-5246-1088-3 (e)

Print information available on the last page.

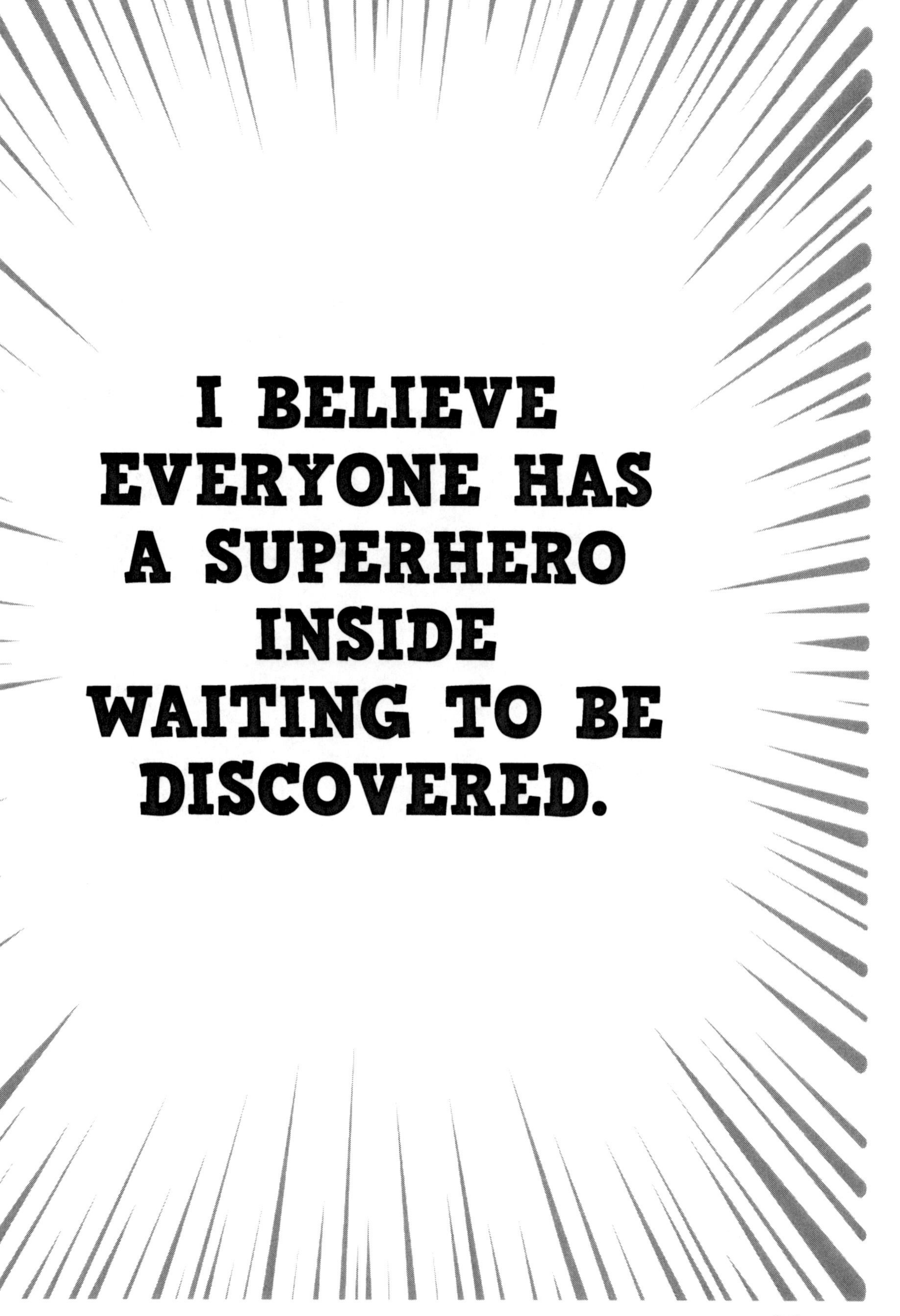
I BELIEVE
EVERYONE HAS
A SUPERHERO
INSIDE
WAITING TO BE
DISCOVERED.

IN THIS BOOK YOU WILL LEARN HOW TO FIND YOUR INNER SUPERHERO THROUGH IGNITING YOUR SUPERPOWERS.

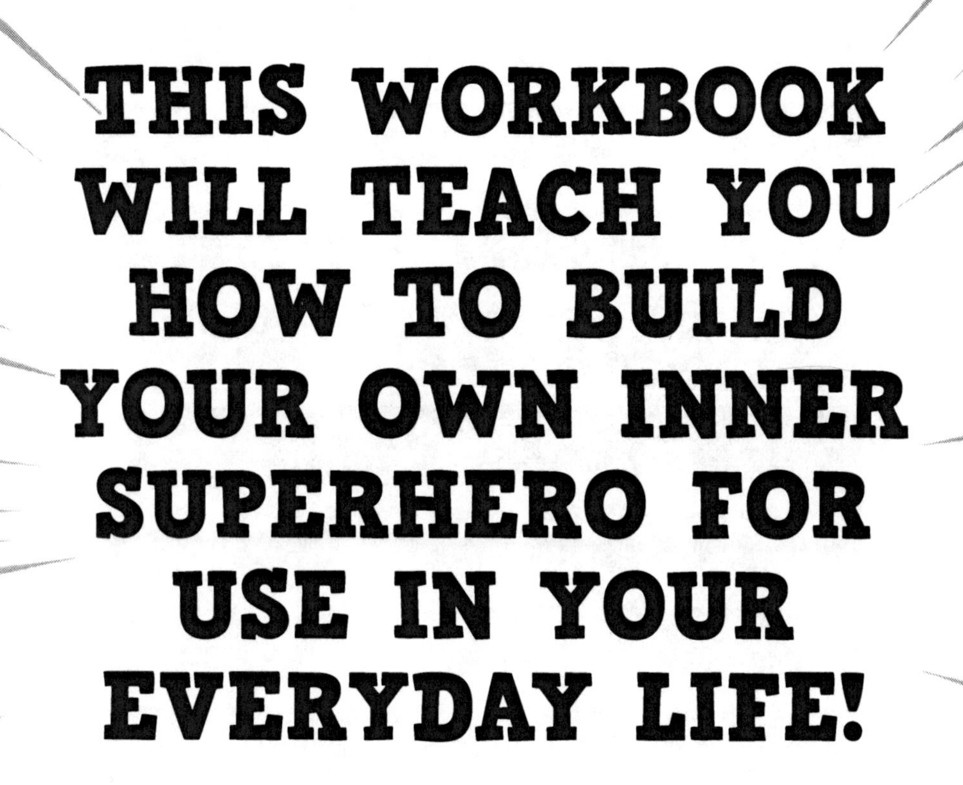
THIS WORKBOOK
WILL TEACH YOU
HOW TO BUILD
YOUR OWN INNER
SUPERHERO FOR
USE IN YOUR
EVERYDAY LIFE!

BY THE END OF THIS WORKBOOK YOU WILL CREATE A SUPERHERO PLEDGE WHICH IS YOUR CODE TO LIVE BY TO FULFILL YOUR SUPERHERO MISSIONS.

THE CODE YOU CREATE WILL GUIDE YOU THROUGH UNDERSTANDING HOW TO THRIVE AS A STUDENT. YOU WILL LEARN TO OVERCOME PEER PRESSURE, NEGATIVE THINKING, AND BULLYING BY BUILDING SELF ESTEEM, CONFIDENCE, AND PERSONAL POWER. YOU WILL BUILD THESE LIFE SKILLS BY TAPPING INTO YOUR INNER SUPERHERO. I WILL PROVIDE YOU WITH AN OUTLINE TO DO THIS. YOU WILL FEEL THE POWER BY ENGAGING IN THE WORKBOOK ACTIVITES AND PARTICIPATING IN YOUR INNER SUPERHERO GROWTH CHALLENGES. I AM SHARING WITH YOU STORIES, FORMULAS, AND ACTIVITIES THAT I HAVE USED TO AWAKEN MY OWN INNER SUPERHERO. THIS PROCESS SAVED MY OWN LIFE AND BROUGHT TO LIFE MY DREAMS AS WELL AS OTHERS' DREAMS!

ARE YOU READY?

TOP SECRET MISSION

Only serious students who are ready to awaken their inner superhero please read forward

A MESSAGE FROM THE AUTHOR

I WROTE THIS BOOK FOR ONE MAIN PURPOSE - TO SAVE AND TRANSFORM THE LIVES OF OTHERS. I AIM TO PROVIDE EDUCATION, KNOWLEDGE, TOOLS, SUPPORT, AND WISDOM THAT STUDENTS, PARENTS, EDUCATORS, AND PROFESSIONALS CAN EASILY APPLY TO SCHOOL AND LIFE.

ONE OF MY PERSONAL SUPERHERO MISSIONS IS TO WORK WITH PEOPLE WHO HAVE EXPERIENCED PAIN FROM FEELING STUCK WITH PAST LIFE EVENTS BECAUSE THEY DIDN'T KNOW HOW TO DEAL WITH THEM. THIS MAY HAVE RESULTED IN NEGATIVE THINKING, DEPRESSION, AND ANXIETY. THIS PAIN MAY HAVE LED TO SUICIDAL THOUGHTS AND UNHEALTHY LIVING.

MY PURPOSE IS TO REACH THOSE IN NEED BY PROVIDING THE TOOLS AND INFORMATION NECESSARY TO TRANSFORM THEIR LIVES FROM NEGATIVE TO POSITIVE.

PERSONALLY, I STRUGGLED THROUGH MY SCHOOL DAYS AND ALMOST DIDN'T MAKE IT OUT ALIVE. THIS IS WHY I HAVE DEDICATED MY LIFE TO SHARING MY STORY TO INSPIRE OTHERS WHO WANT TO LEARN HOW TO BETTER UNDERSTAND THEMSELVES, TO INTEGRATE THIS SELF-KNOWLEDGE, AND TO NAVIGATE WITH STRENGTH THROUGH THEIR SCHOOL DAYS.

MY PASSION IS TO RAISE AWARENESS OF PHYSICAL HEALTH, EMOTIONAL HEALTH, MENTAL HEALTH, AND SPIRITUAL HEALTH SO THAT STUDENTS MAY BEGIN TO FEEL COMFORTABLE TALKING ABOUT CHALLENGES AT SCHOOL AND AT HOME.

I DEDICATE THIS WORKBOOK TO STUDENTS, TEACHERS, EDUCATORS, PARENTS, HEALTH CARE PROFESSIONALS, COUNSELORS, AND THERAPISTS. MAY THIS BOOK GIVE YOU LIFE-CHANGING TOOLS AND ACTIVITIES TO USE AS YOU ARE EMPOWERED OR AS YOU EMPOWER OTHERS WHO READ THIS BOOK TO GROW THROUGH SCHOOL CHALLENGES AND ACHIEVE LIFELONG DREAMS.

"EMPOWERING STUDENTS TODAY TO BUILD BRIGHT FUTURES FOR TOMORROW"

I DEDICATE THIS BOOK TO

MY INCREDIBLE MOTHER FOR ALL THE AMAZING CHOICES AND DECISIONS YOU MADE FOR OUR FAMILY!

THANK YOU FOR YOUR COMMITTMENT TO GO ON THIS HEALING JOURNEY WITH ME!

THANK YOU FOR SUPPORTING ME DURING SCHOOL, THROUGH MY THERAPY, BY ATTENDING EVENTS, BY CREATING VIDEOS, THROUGH YOUR UNCONDITIONAL LOVE, AND MANY MANY MANY MORE THINGS! I AM SO HAPPY AND GREATEFUL THAT YOU ARE MY MOM!

THE BEST IS YET TO COME FOR US:)

P.S: I LOVE YOU MORE!!!

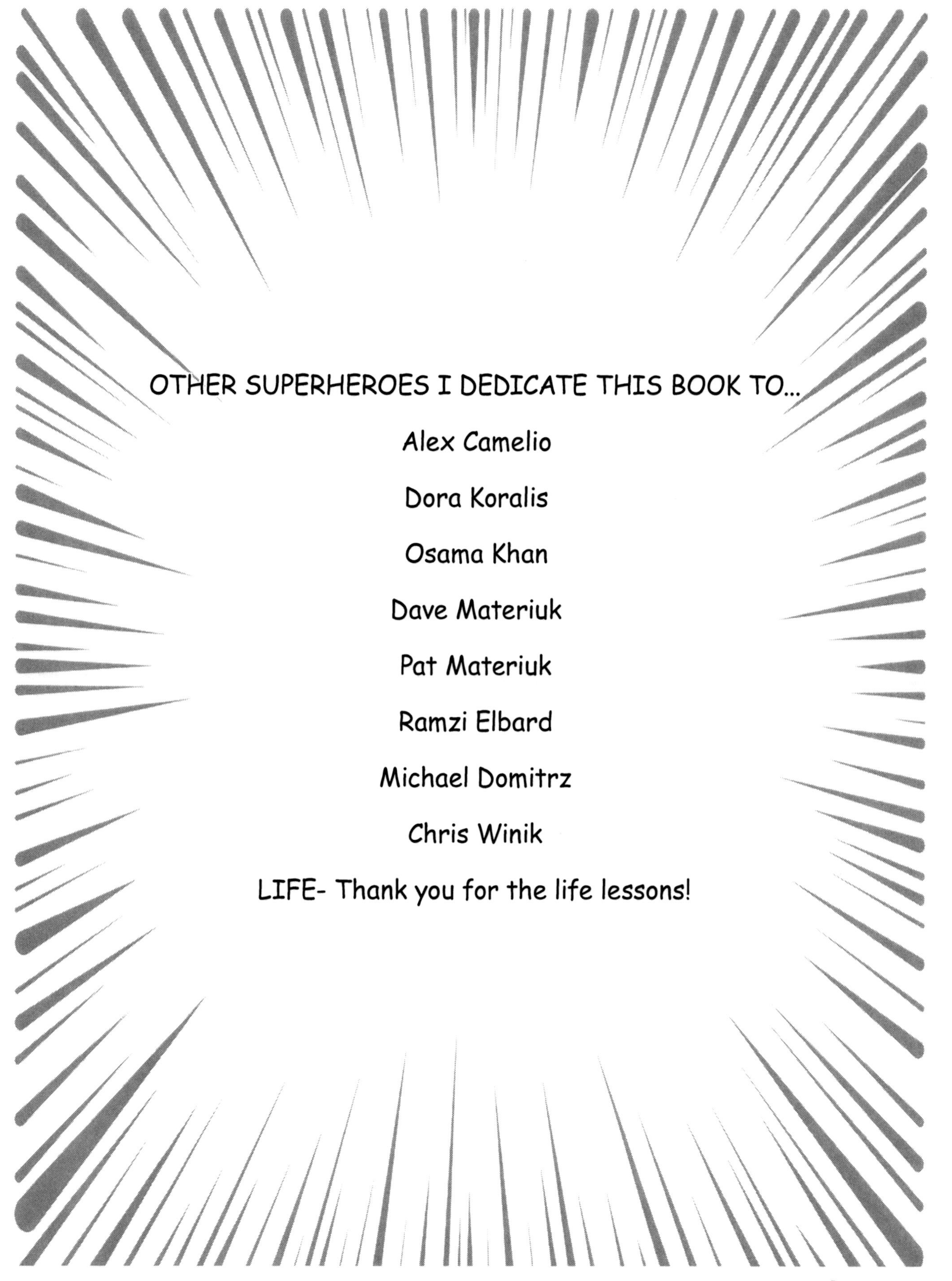

OTHER SUPERHEROES I DEDICATE THIS BOOK TO...

Alex Camelio

Dora Koralis

Osama Khan

Dave Materiuk

Pat Materiuk

Ramzi Elbard

Michael Domitrz

Chris Winik

LIFE- Thank you for the life lessons!

Special Thanks to the Maitland Street
Residence Group Home.
I wouldn't be where I am today without
the Group Home experience.

"WE ALL HAVE LIFE WORK TO ACCOMPLISH IN THIS LIFETIME. ARE YOU AWARE OF YOUR LIFE WORK?"

The greatest expression of gratitude one can feel is paying forward teachings that have saved and enhanced the quality of others' lives.

-Erica Humphrey

Table of Contents

Part 1 - Inner Superhero VS Inner Villain

Part 2 - How to POWER Up your Inner Superhero

POWER

The Power of This Workbook!

My goal and focus with this workbook is to grab your attention by sparking excitement with a fun superhero theme and superhero activities. I want to share how much FUN it can be for you to build your own life skills. These life skills are so valuable. Not only will these life skills serve you well as you graduate through the school years, but you will find that these life skills will continue to serve you well in your ordinary everyday life after school!

Together, we will ignite your inner superhero. You will be fed valuable life skills which you can implement to overcome school and life challenges through recognizing your superhero missions.

This is a process that lasts a lifetime!

This process is sooo powerful that I feel it would be uncool not to share it with you. You will witness the power of awakening your inner superhero through reading stories, participating in activities, developing solutions, brainstorming, and engaging in your inner superhero growth challenges. Through this process, you will come to realize that you've had this power all along. You will understand that everyone has the potential to feel this power to overcome any life challenge and achieve any life dream. I dedicate this book to you and your life journey. You are important. You are special. You have a life purpose. I challenge you to be brave, bold, courageous, honest, open-minded, and flexible as you follow through on your word and the actions in this book. I am giving you the straight goods. I am sharing exactly what worked for me to overcome my school and life challenges. Remember, the POWER comes from doing the activities in this book. When you do the activities, you will find, build, and develop your own inner superhero, if you haven't found it already. If you have already found your inner superhero, then these activities will serve to enhance the strength of your inner superhero.

At the end of the day, you will be able to use your superhero to achieve your life's mission and life's purpose through overcoming challenges. My intention is to empower you. I want you to see that you have the power to live your bestest, coolest, most awesome life. Sound good?

The Power is in Taking Action

Learning how to awaken your inner superhero is by far the best life lesson I have learned, and it is best learned through taking massive amounts of action. I can share all the stories and knowledge in the world, but the truth is that nothing in your life will truly change until you take action. This is why I have purposefully given you personal growth activities, challenges, formulas, and brainstorming sessions. I am sharing these with you because it is through these activities that you will awaken or enhance the awakening of your inner superhero.

I know that you may be wondering what I mean by your inner superhero. Keep reading, and I will show you...

SUPERHEROES ARE EVERYWHERE!

BAM

Let's start with the basics

What is the world's greatest Superhero Story? When you think of real life superhero stories, who do you think of? Do you think of Gandhi, the leader of the Indian independence movement in British-ruled India? By employing nonviolent civil disobedience, Gandhi led India to independence and inspired movements for civil rights and freedom across the world. Or how about Mother Teresa, who believed in wholehearted free service to the poorest of the poor? Her work reached over 133 countries where she was responsible for running hospices and homes for people with HIV/AIDS, leprosy and tuberculosis; soup kitchens; dispensaries and mobile clinics; children's and family counselling programs; orphanages; and schools. How about Nelson Mandela, who served as President of South Africa from 1994 to 1999? He was the country's first black chief executive. Or how about Martin Luther King, best known for his role in the advancement of civil rights using nonviolent civil disobedience? And don't forget Oprah Winfrey, American media proprietor, talk show host, actress, producer, and philanthropist. She is best known for her talk show The Oprah Winfrey Show, which was the highest-rated program of its kind in history and was nationally syndicated from 1986 to 2011. Dubbed the "Queen of All Media", she has been ranked the richest African-American of the 20th century. What makes up the qualities of a superhero? Is it leadership, empowering others, communication, honesty, passion, resiliency, saving lives, and changing the quality of life for others? I could go on and on talking about the amazing superheroes who have walked this planet!

I think superheroes can be and are people who live the normal day-to-day life, like my mom for example. For many reasons, my mom is one of my superheroes. I definitely wouldn't be where I am today without her!

As a child growing up, we hear stories of superheroes like Batman saving Gotham, or the Avengers working together as a team to conquer evil. How about Daredevil, the man without fear; or Man of Steel, saving the lives of others with his power of flight?

Traditionally, we are taught that superheroes exist outside of ourselves. We believe that some other person is going to come in to save the day. But what if that person doesn't show up and you need saving? What will you do? How will you be saved, or how will your situation be solved?

For starters, do you know that everyone has a superhero inside of them? Yes, that is right! You have the potential and personal power to ignite and unleash your inner superhero to rise up and save your day! Your inner superhero can solve your problems, achieve your life's goals and dreams, and learn how to work with other superheroes.

How does one tap into their personal power? How does one ignite or unleash this inner superhero and superpowers?

I am confident that some of you who are reading this book have already started using some of your natural born gifts for greatness. I know that some of you have already released your inner superhero, and it is awake!

This book is for all people who are looking to build, enhance, and take their superhero's inner strength to the next level, no matter where you are at in school or life.

By engaging in this workbook, my goal is for you to realize that the best superhero story in the world will be your own story.

Imagine if everyone were to wake up to this truth? How will this world be different? Imagine if there were more Gandhi's, Mother Teresa's, Martin Luther King's, and Oprahs in the world? What would our world look like?

Why do we feel we need a superhero?

Where does this feeling come from? I believe that there are a few core reasons why people look for superheroes. First, I think we as human beings have lost touch with knowing our own personal power. (We often feel powerless in life to solve our own needs. We think someone else needs to do it for us.) Second, I truly believe that we are naturally designed for growth, so we look to learn from others to provide the answers we are searching for. We look for role models, coaches, and awesome people to learn from! Like the Avengers, we can create teams and learn from all people and experiences that come in and out of our lives - no matter who or what they are.

Let's face it: school and life can be challenging. We all have needs as human beings, and when these needs are not met, life can feel scary. We look outside of ourselves to solve the problems, but the reality is we can only solve our problems by first going within ourselves.

What is the opposite of a superhero?

I have come to learn that life has a balance of opposites. For example, I know that there is positive and negative, light and dark, right and wrong, female and male, etc. So what is the opposite of a superhero? The opposite of a superhero is a villain. What is a villain? A villain is a person who doesn't necessarily have evil motives but their behaviour can hurt others. I truly believe that there is only a small number of evil people in the world with truly evil motives who take action to hurt others for personal gain. A villain is a person who uses their superpowers for evil to hurt others around them. I believe that even villains have inner superheroes, but they've connected and aligned more with their inner villain. Their inner villain has more power. Even so, I feel that these people are lost in life. I believe that villains are afraid. I believe that even villains are searching for their inner superhero. I believe it is the inner superheroes of others that can lead the transformation of villains into superheroes. Villains are terrorists. Villains are people who hurt, kill, and destroy the lives of others and ultimately themselves. In the superhero world, villains are beings like Mr. Freeze, Doctor Octopus, Poison Ivy, or the Riddler.

I believe everyone has an inner villain and an inner superhero.

Which side becomes stronger? Which side is more powerful? Well, it's the side that you give the most attention to. It's the side of you that feels more empowered, the side that makes most of the decisions, actions, and statements. When we ignite our inner superhero, we are able to stand up against our inner villain to protect against negative living such as negative thinking or bullying. In this way, we can overcome peer pressure. Our inner superhero has the power to show the inner villain how to finally join the inner superhero to become one. Our inner superhero knows what true power is. I believe that the inner villain has great strengths and superpowers, but uses them to hurt themselves and others. When the inner superhero and inner villain become friends and work together, then TRUE greatness can be achieved.

When you wake up your inner superhero and do the necessary life work, you will reach a point where there is no more inward bullying, destructive self talk, or negativity. With this transformation all thoughts and emotions are aligned in a healthy happy state of being ready to take on the world with a new collaboration of superpowers! The aftermath of the inner villain and inner superhero working towards becoming one is high levels of self esteem, confidence, personal power, positive thinking, and healthy living which in turn shines brightly onto others. This is a process and takes time; however, it is the most rewarding process any human being can undergo in this life.

How did I realize that I could be my own superhero?

I was uncomfortable being present in the moment. I was often looking to escape the present moment and frequently found myself wanting to be somewhere else. If you are like me and know the feeling of waiting, then you'll get this piece. In my life I was waiting. I was waiting for my feelings to change, and for my life events and lifestyle to change. In school, I was expecting some dream boy to come sweep me off my feet; I was waiting for good grades; I was waiting for my parents to build a relationship with me; I was waiting for new friends to enter my life; I was waiting for my body to change; I was waiting for my living situation to change. I was waiting for direction on where to take my life after school, etc., etc., etc. - You fill in the blanks. I think you get what I mean.

What was I really waiting for?

Basically, I was waiting for a "superhero person" to come save me and give me the life I wanted. I was waiting for that person or opportunity to magically show up in my life to give me the life that I was dreaming of.

What I was really waiting for was for ME to show up to be my own superhero.

When I was 21 I experienced an awakening that changed my life forever. I realized all that waiting was for me, my inner superhero, to stand up to my inner villain. This finally resulted in me saving my own life!

"I was waiting for me to step up and be my own superhero."

In stepping up to BE the person I was looking for, I began to discover I had possessed the powers all along. I could use these superpowers to solve my own inner needs of love, sense of belonging, confidence, self esteem, attention, relationships, scholarships, good grades, healthy living, and just pure awesomeness!

What exactly is our inner superhero?

You have probably figured it out by now. Your inner superhero is your greatness, your personal power, your inner wisdom, etc. At the core, your inner superhero is a presence within you. Your inner superhero is full of so many amazing energies including love, joy, compassion, strength, courage, vulnerability, truth, and awesomeness! This presence is self-aware, real, honest, secure, and understands why you make decisions the way you do. This presence is a fearless leader full of courage and power. This presence has the power to turn negativity into positivity and to see challenges as opportunities to grow. This presence is an opportunity seeker with the power to overcome any life event, challenge, and crisis.

One of my Superheroes who found her inner superhero is Louise Hay!

Have you heard of Louise Hay? She is another one of my superheroes and for many reasons! She has fantastic books on positivity, health, love and healing. I particularly LOVE her books on affirmations. In her book *Heal your Life* she discusses how she healed herself from cancer with the power of thought. You can't see the wind, but you can see the effects it has on the environment. The same applies for positive thinking. Positive thinking is an energy vibration that attracts similar people, experiences, and environment conditions. Thinking positive and expecting the best will attract more positive in your life. In Louise's case she was able to heal herself from cancer. I think her story sums up how powerful positive thinking can be!

I want you to know that the power to heal and the power of positivity is the same presence that I am discussing here. The inner superhero has the power to heal and eradicate any self doubt/self esteem issues or negative thought patterns that are causing harm in your life. The inner superhero has the power to build self love, self esteem, confidence, self respect, love, and happiness. The inner superhero has the power to forgive others, no matter what action has been done. The inner superhero is capable of breaking down the inner walls and taking the appropriate action to create the solutions needed to solve problems and achieve desired life dreams. I believe that every human being has an inner superhero just waiting to be discovered.

How do you know when your inner superhero is awake?

You know your superhero is awake when you find yourself listening to thoughts that are aligned with love, kindness, compassion, and truth. Your inner superhero wants to guide you to live your life full of health, love, joy, and purpose. Every human being is born for a unique life purpose that is special to their individual desires for growth. Your inner superhero is aware of this purpose and guides you through life. Some people call this knowing an intuition or conscience. Either way, your inner superhero loves you unconditionally and has wisdom that can guide you to overcome any life challenge and achieve any life dream. This means that every single human being who is born has a destiny. Your inner superhero is here for you - no matter what happens. NO MATTER WHAT! Your inner superhero wants to protect you and save you from your inner villain, negative self talk, inner bully, and other villains that you may come across in your life that may say or do mean or hurtful things. Your inner superhero will teach you how to deal with life challenges and clear the path for you against villains to live a healthy and happy life. Your inner superhero will show you how to turn those pains into superpowers - to see the life lessons in life experiences.

Awakening your superhero is like building a relationship. The more you listen, pay attention, and take the appropriate actions in line with your life's purpose, the more powerful your inner superhero becomes.

How do you build a relationship with your inner superhero so that it will support you?

Beginning a relationship with your inner superhero means that you have begun the journey to uncovering and discovering who you are. On the journey of discovering who you are, what naturally unfolds depends on the individual; however, commonly you will see your life's mission, purpose, core values, relationships, personality traits, areas of growth, opportunities, strengths, and passions.

"People come into our lives for a reason, for a season, or for a lifetime."

You have a burning desire to learn and study your life and the people in your life. You recognize and celebrate your superpowers (unique gifts, talents, abilities, and skills) both in yourself and in others. You know life is not perfect and you don't expect it to be, but you expect growth. You look for the positive within others and within life's situations because you understand the power of attention and focus of thoughts in creating a happy and healthy lifestyle. You understand the power of leadership and empowering others, and you know how this builds your personal confidence and success in school and in life. You know when to let go of things, when to forgive, when to be the leader, when to accept events in your life, and when to rise up to achieve your greatness! You understand that people flow in and out of your life for a purpose and you choose to see the teachings. Building a relationship with your inner superhero is a process, and it all begins with believing and acknowledging that the power exists within you to wake it up.

"I am open and flexible to personal growth in life."

"SCHOOL DAYS CAN BE TOUGH. WHAT TOOLS DO YOU HAVE TO OVERCOME CHALLENGES AND ACHIEVE YOUR DREAMS?"

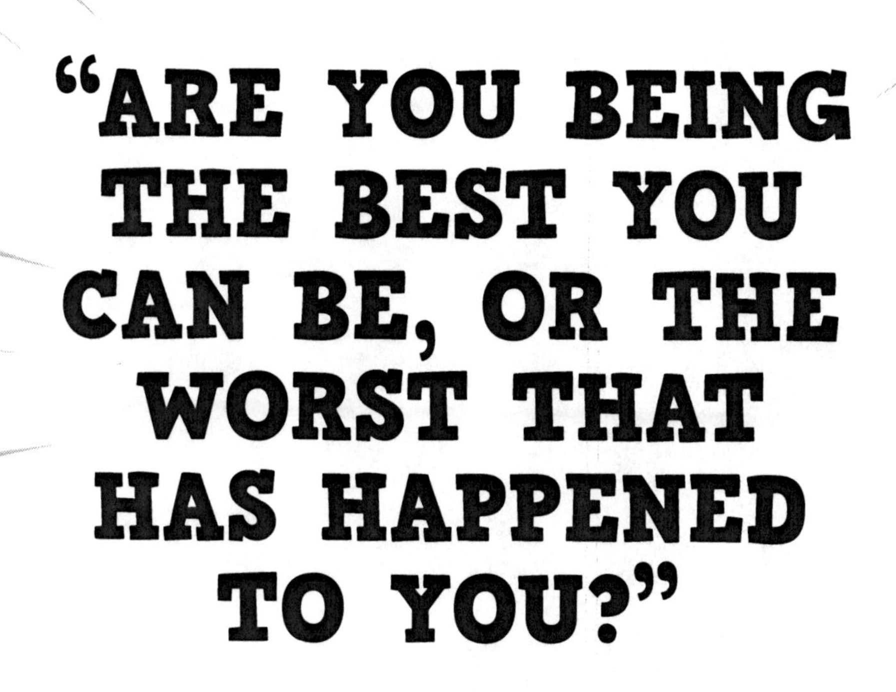
"ARE YOU BEING
THE BEST YOU
CAN BE, OR THE
WORST THAT
HAS HAPPENED
TO YOU?"

Part 1: Inner Superhero Vs. Inner Villain

Erica's STORY

"Sometimes we get lost before we find ourselves."

Allow Me to be Straight Up with You.

Allow me to officially introduce myself. My name is Erica Humphrey. I am a Motivational Speaker/Award-Winning Fitness Professional and Life Coach. I wrote this book because I saved my own life through finding and releasing my inner superhero. As a result, I have felt a deep burning desire and inspiration to share my story with you and with as many people as possible on how to awaken their inner superhero.

"How I got into public speaking"

I am inspired to share my story with you because I was sought out in my early 20s by an amazing teacher to speak about my experiences. I was asked to share how I achieved my accomplishments with the goal of inspiring students that anything is possible.

I know firsthand the challenges of growing up. I think that the student years are the most challenging and important because you are building your foundation. You are figuring out who you are, who you want to be, and what you want to do with your life. With the influences, pressures, and societal expectations in school, many students get lost. I was lost. When we are lost, we often look outside of ourselves to find the answers. But the truth is we must look within, because that is where we will find the answers.

I am going to get REAL with you!

***Before I get real with you I want to be crystal clear here, as my childhood wasn't all "bad" - though it was challenging. There were many great memories and moments that my family created. However, because of my mindset back then, the challenges outweighed the positive. In the beginning, I was worse in my actions and behaviour because of what had happened to me. *** My personal story begins mainly from the viewpoint of the inner villain. You will see that after the awakening my view began to change. I began to see life through the eyes of my inner superhero.

Note: igniting and awakening your inner superhero is a process that takes time. It is important we be patient with ourselves and find ways to enjoy the process.

"The truth set me free"

I am not going to sugarcoat my story, life events, or feelings. Why should I? I believe in speaking the truth. It is the truth that set me free from my inner villain (the inner pain in my life). Therefore, I am passionate in talking about painful issues because this discussion brings awareness and empowers the solutions. Speaking my own truth and asking for others to speak their truth was and still is a catalyst of change for me. The truth has literally set me free from my internal suffering that I created and experienced. So I know firsthand the power of truth and of being honest. That is what you can expect from me. As a speaker and life teacher I promise to be straightforward and honest with you - no BS :) - because it takes honesty to overcome challenges and achieve your life goals and dreams.

Alright, are you ready to read a story of trials, tribulations, and triumphs? That is what my story is. It isn't always pretty, but it is real. I share my story in hopes of inspiring others to overcome life challenges and achieve life dreams!

"We are all dealt a hand of cards in life. It is not what we are dealt that determines our destiny; it is how we play those cards."

I had to learn how to play the cards that I was dealt. I had to learn how to look for opportunities to set myself up for success and play the best game of my life. My story has multiple stages of growth periods and what I call building blocks toward releasing my inner pain through igniting my inner superhero. I will share and highlight the activities in multiple building blocks, from one stage to another. I want to be as crystal clear as possible with you on what I went through and what activities led to awakening my inner superhero. Sound good? :)

ALRIGHT, LET'S DO THIS!

"We are all born into a life cycle. I believe every single being is born for a life purpose and born into a culture/society with a set of beliefs to live a certain way. I believe these experiences are a part of our life plan and life growth."

Allow me to share with you my upbringing and childhood experiences. I was born in Woodstock, Ontario, Canada as the eldest child in my family with two younger brothers. I was born into a cycle of abuse, addictions, negative thinking, low levels of self esteem/confidence, and poverty. My parents were unconscious and unaware in their thinking and behaviour. They were unaware of their thoughts and lifestyle. When I say I was born into a cycle, I am referring to the quality of lifestyle that I was born into including attitudes, beliefs, and behaviours.

You see, these attitudes, beliefs, and behaviours were passed down a lifecycle from their own parents through unconscious thinking. Often they didn't think or question whether their attitudes, thought patterns, behaviours, or fears were something they wanted to pass down in turn to their own children and others. In this life cycle that had been passed down for generations, the inner villain had more power. My parents were often thinking with their inner villain. At a very young age, I witnessed the effects of low self esteem, low confidence, negative thinking, and bullying. I witnessed what it was like to live in survival mode and in fear. My parents had been passed down a lifecycle that needed healing.

In a nutshell, my father was a bully. He was mean, hurtful, and damaging to my mother's self esteem. My mother struggled with standing up for herself because of her low self esteem and lack of confidence. Please know that my parents were great on many levels, and that was when their inner superheroes shone through! We would go on weekend trips; engage in sports, crafts, and baking; and play outdoors with our dogs! We would laugh, dress up for holidays, watch funny movies, and spend time together.

The circle of Life!

During the beginning of my life, I adopted my parents' ways of living - most of the time.

Allow me to shed more light on my parents' relationship. For the majority of the time, their relationship was unhealthy, disrespectful, and lacking in love for one another. Their relationship was up and down like a light switch. My dad was dominant, intimidating, and frightening. At times, my dad would yell and throw objects to express his emotions because he didn't know how to deal with his emotions in a healthy way. My dad would verbally and emotionally abuse my mom. As a result, my mom lived with anxiety which eventually developed into depression. My mom would worry, focus on the negative, and think the worst was going to happen because of the abuse she went through. Both parents struggled with communication skills. I know deep down they wanted to heal from the negativity, but didn't know how to deal with their emotions or life events. The inner superhero was searching for the answers.

Typical Gender Roles Back Then

In my parents' generation it was more common for the man to work and the woman to stay home most of the time if not all the time. So my mom was financially dependent on my dad. When my dad was physically, mentally, emotionally, and spiritually abusive to her and she wanted to leave, she didn't have many options on where to go other than the local women's shelter. My mom did what she had to do to feel safe from my dad and protect us, so off we would go. **I have posted a video on YouTube of my mom talking about the women's shelter**

experience. If you interested, please watch. https://www.youtube.com/watch?v=lQWUgGIXaVo

The life of an abusive relationship cycle

But then my parents gave their relationship another go. I truly know deep down that they wanted it to work but didn't know how. Because my parents didn't have the positive life education they needed, they often got stuck in the same unhealthy relationship patterns in a perpetual cycle. They would fight and then get back together, and then fight again. As a result, we went back to the women's shelter for a second time.

I think my mom always thought that my dad would get his stuff together. I think that she truly wanted to believe that he had changed, but the cycle kept repeating itself. I look back now and look at my mom in AWE about how strong she was to make the choice to leave my dad. She went back because she wanted all of us to be together as a family. My mom is such a strong human being! She is one of my superheroes.

I believe that no one enters into a marriage wondering how to mess it up! This cycle was hard on everyone who was involved and is still hard on some of my family members today.

Our parents' relationship is our first introduction to what a relationship means.

The only role model partner relationship I knew back then was my parents. I watched them break up and get back together repeatedly. This pattern affected the health of the relationships I chose later on in life because I was unconsciously repeating the same pattern. This was the only way of living I had in my conscious way of thinking, until I woke up my inner superhero.

I was a Copy Cat Growing Up! Aren't most of us?

Growing up, children are thirsty for knowledge. We look to learn how to be, how to fit in, how to feel wanted, how to be accepted, and how to foster a sense of belonging. The desire to feel loved is so strong that sometimes we embody negative behaviours to fulfill our needs. I believe we do this without knowing our behaviours are negative because this is all that we know. Or we may be aware of our negative behaviours but don't know how else to fulfill our needs. Sometimes we are scared of not knowing how to live life. (If that is the case for you, then I can't wait to share with you the superpower building block section!)

As I was developing as a child, I learned and embodied my family environment. I was a product of my upbringing. Therefore, being around alcohol and watching my mom's fears and reactions to my dad's negativity of abuse led me to feel scared, lost, insecure, and confused.

I took my parents' struggles very personally and thought that there was something wrong with me. My parents struggled with showing how to love because they struggled with loving themselves and each other. So I grew up struggling with loving myself and others. How could my parents possibly teach me something that they themselves did not know? Later I would learn that I have the personal power within me to naturally guide myself to places, people, and environments where I would understand how to develop life skills - regardless of what family dynamic I was born into.

But at the time, I allowed my parents' struggles to be a part of my identity (self esteem) and how I viewed the world. As a result of the environment that I lived in, I didn't believe I was worthy of love. I thought that I wasn't deserving of health, happiness, or respect because I didn't see it at home. I didn't experience it as a child. I didn't know there was another option or another way of living. I simply didn't know the truth. The truth is that *we are all deserving of love, health, happiness, and care no matter what family or life situation we are born into.*

How has your childhood affected your day-to-day life?

How has your parents' relationship impacted you today? As I write this story, I reflect and remember that the experiences that happen in our childhood continue to impact us today. When we have been hurt by others but don't release the hurt, let it go, or see the love intention behind it, we often play out that same hurt or experience with someone else. For true healing to occur, we must see past others' pains. We must take the lead on behaving in a healthy way, so that we don't pass on that hurt to someone else. We know how it feels to be hurt. So why would we want someone else to feel that?!

Or maybe your experience with your parents was different than mine. Maybe your parents figured life out and knew how to live a healthy and happy marriage. Maybe you were passed down a different life cycle. Whatever your story or case may be, I challenge you to be a leader to others in terms of living a healthy life. I invite you to consciously choose to enter into and create healthy relationships. You deserve it!

I challenge others to consciously choose to be the change they want to be in the world - NO MATTER WHAT!

Life Growing Pains

As I was growing up I experienced a lot of growing pains. I was unsure of myself and struggled with making friendships and communicating with others. I had a hard time knowing how to deal with my emotions. In fact, my emotions usually controlled me. I would act out impulsively without thinking rationally. I didn't enjoy going to school because I had a hard time focusing on the task at hand (I couldn't be present in the moment) which sometimes put me behind. I got pulled into "special" classes because my learning wasn't up to speed with the majority. My day-to-day living was a challenge because I was consumed with negative thinking and distracted by fearful thoughts, worry, and anxiety. I felt alone, shy, and scared to live life every day. I experienced negative thinking because I had low self esteem, low self worth, and low self respect. As a result, I was easily influenced by peer pressures including bullying (being bullied and bullying others) and skipping school. At this time in my life my inner villain had more power.

A Big Moment for Everyone Involved

As I mentioned, my parents separated multiple times. Eventually there was one final separation which ultimately led to their divorce. During this final break up their drama directly impacted me, because I was influenced to make a decision.

Parents' Messy Separation Divided the Family

I didn't want my parents to split up. They were my parents! All I wanted was to be with the two people who had created me and feel their love under one roof! But my parents' separation was out of my control, and it was decided that my dad was moving out. My dad asked me to live with him, and because I didn't want to hurt my dad's feelings, I said yes without thinking of my mom's reaction. My dad asked me to call my mom to tell her that I wasn't coming home. My mom came to my dad's place and fought hard to get me to come with her. It was like a tug of war between my parents. They were both calling my name and telling me to do two different things and I didn't know what to do. This situation was highly emotional. I was so afraid that I ran upstairs to hide and cry. I was afraid to hurt my dad's feelings, and was trusting him to work things out with my mom. My dream was to live part-time at my dad's and part-time at my mom's. But when I came downstairs, my mom and dad were gone. This life event caused tremendous pain between my mom, my dad, me, and my brothers. My brothers lived with my mom and were now without a sister living at home.

Both of my parents wanted custody and fought for me. My mom fought hard and hired an attorney. Out of fear, low self esteem, and lack of confidence I decided to stay living with my dad - even though

I wanted to go back home with my mom. I didn't know how to deal. I believe this is when my inner villain started to become stronger.

I felt powerless, helpless, and stuck in life with this past event. My inner villain started to grow.

I began to feel emotions of abandonment. Although my dad had asked me to come live with him, he was rarely home. I remember thinking: "Dad, why did you ask me to come live with you when you are not even here to spend time with me?" My dad worked a lot. He always had great work ethic. But I remember wondering why he had asked me to come live with him if he was going to work all the time. Did he expect me to raise myself?

At this point I rarely talked to my mom or my brothers. My dad was never home. So, I felt I had no choice but to raise myself. I had to care for my own physical and emotional needs. At 12 I was doing my own cooking and cleaning. I dealt with my female milestones alone. I was forced to deal with life events and situations by myself. For guidance I basically observed what my friends or the other kids at school were doing. I observed TV shows, movies, and music to decide how to be, how to dress, how to talk, and how to fit in with others through these influences. As time went on, I began to be angry and sad because I felt alone and scared. I started to become someone I wasn't.

"I was starting to feed into my inner villain."

I felt I wasn't worthy of love because my dad wasn't spending time with me, and because my mom and I were not talking very often. I wasn't sure how to handle my emotional pain of dealing with my parents' separation all while trying to figure out school, who I was, and who I wanted to be. I felt lost and confused. I was desperate for attention, love, and acceptance. I just wanted to feel loved and receive attention!!!

I didn't know this then, but this life event was only the beginning of more pain in my life. I had unfinished business including anger, hurt, resentment, abandonment issues, not trusting people, etc. with this life event for many years. I later cleared up my unfinished business with this event through communication, acceptance, looking for the positive, and forgiveness. (Look for more on these topics in the building blocks section!)

MY INNER SUPERHERO WAS SLEEPING

Life moves on with or without you

Grades 6, 7, and 8

I call these years the character building years. These are the years when we begin formulating our self perception and our opinion of ourselves. This is when we begin to make important life decisions that set us up for the future teen years. We begin to develop independence through progressing through the school grades and life. We begin to exercise our free choice and free will as we are given more power to make decisions while growing up. These are fundamental years that need careful guidance.

I had a chip on my shoulder and it wasn't coming off.

It was during these years that I was living with my dad. Since my dad was working to support us and he wasn't home very often, I didn't have rules, expectations, tough love, or structure. Even if he did give rules, he wasn't home to enforce them or check up on me.

Maybe some of you can relate: I felt alone and isolated because although a part of me wanted to talk about my life problems, I didn't know how.

Another part of me was embarrassed and scared to talk about my life challenges. I saw talking about my problems as a weakness and not as a sign of strength. I thought life was supposed to be perfect and I knew mine wasn't. I thought there was something wrong with me. I didn't know that life was about growth.

I saw other families that seemed to have everything together and wondered why mine didn't. (I didn't see the truth - that life is growth. I didn't know that some life experiences were out of my control in terms of how other people acted, but I could still control my behaviour and responses. For example, I could have spoken up to my parents and communicated my needs, asked for help, or kept myself busy with extracurricular activities to occupy me until I was older.)

Back then I didn't see the growth opportunities in these life situations. All I saw was the negative which held me back from moving forward to developing a life of happiness and healthy living. My negative thinking, worrying, and fears were creating more negative in my life. For a long time, I carried my pain, sadness, and fear with me everywhere I went. I was scared. I didn't know how to be or how to deal with these life situations that seemed to be unfolding fast in front of me. I would expect the worst. I would visualize negative experiences happening like not having any friends, not having a relationship with my mom, and being stuck with these low energies and negative emotions forever.

When I look back on my school days of growing through grades 6, 7, and 8, I realize that there are three HOT topics that I didn't know how to deal with. Knowing how to deal with these topics could have been a life changer for me.

These hot topics are BULLYING, PEER PRESSURE, and NEGATIVE THINKING

My inner villain of bullying was growing.

I wasn't aware of this then, but my inner self talk was negative. I felt sad, angry, and depressed. I was filled with uncertainty and anxiety. I was scared of the future - what would or could happen next - and I was depressed from past events. I was beating myself up for what had happened in the past, because I was taking life events personally. This affected my mental, emotional, and physical health. I felt scared to live life.

I was a BULLY TO ME.

What took me a while to figure out was that I was being a bully to me. I was beating myself up for what had happened with my parents. I mean, I already had the odds stacked against me through being born into a negative lifecycle of abuse, addictions, and low income. I was struggling with who I was and who I wanted to be. Because I was a bully on the inside, I was a bully on the outside. Later I learned we can only give to others what we have inside of us.

I bullied other girls.

The truth is I did participate in bullying. I would gossip and talk behind people's backs. I would feel jealous and threatened by other girls' looks and styles or by how they got attention. I didn't know this then, but I was insecure and had low levels of self esteem and confidence. I didn't feel good about myself and was scared about that. Since I was a bully to myself through my inner negative talk, it was easy to be a bully to others. At that moment in time, I didn't know that there was another way to be. (My inner superhero wasn't awake yet.)

Later in life, in an effort to strengthen my inner superhero and heal my inner villain, I went out to the people who I hurt. I apologized to them and asked for forgiveness. I am happy and grateful that most people were forgiving and receptive. The ones who weren't were not ready to forgive. That's okay. I did everything in my power, and most importantly I forgave myself.

*** For anyone who I missed during my massive apology challenge, I am going to take this opportunity and send a massive shout out to anyone who I bullied. Will you forgive me? ***

Life is about growth.

The Truth About Bullying

Back then I was mean to others. I judged people. I said things that would hurt them. This was all based on unconscious thinking. I was not self aware. Through awakening my inner superhero, I learned that when we put someone else down, we are putting ourselves down too. Bullying never wins. People bully because they feel insecure about themselves. They feel better when they put someone else down. But the truth is this feeling is only a short term, temporary feeling of power. Bullies are missing the boat! They are missing what true personal power is and how to activate it.

Bullying doesn't give true personal power.

Through my personal journey of self reflection and coaching others about bullying, I've learned that bullies usually feel guilty after they have bullied someone. This behaviour further develops their inner villain.

"Be the Change you want to see in the world."

I believe that bullies are searching for answers on how to behave differently. I believe this because when people are bullies they are hurting on the inside, and I truly believe that people do not want to live with pain. I believe that bullies just don't have the knowledge, education, or tools on how to help their inner bully. Their inner superhero isn't awake yet. If bullies only KNEW differently. If only they knew how much more amazing it feels to use your inner superhero to communicate with others and to build, empower, and love others. Bullies are surely missing out! Let's live life the way of the superhero and show bullies what true personal power is!

To help the inner bully, the inner superhero must be strengthened from within. This can happen when the bully chooses to build self esteem and confidence and heal past pains so that there are no more negative emotions to pass onto others. BE the superhero to show bullies how to behave. Sometimes sharing stories and communicating authentically with others can help. This may open up a door, for the inner bully must see that they've been hurt or are hurting in some way. They must see the life lessons in their past pain. Only in this way can the bully let go, forgive, and feel good on the inside! If you are a victim of bullying, use your inner superhero to show bullies how to interact with others through living by example.

Note: Don't be shy to talk to someone about bullying! It is way too common these days and a lot of people have already gone through it or are going through it right now. Approach someone you trust like your parents, teachers, or therapist.

How to respond to bullies

* Be the person you want the bully to be. Show them how through demonstrating and being the example.

* Immediately forgive the bully (you forgive for you and them). Know that what you are seeing is their inner villain, not their inner superhero. They are showing you their past pain, and how they were treated before. They must be shown another way to be. They must be shown the rewards of aligning with their inner superhero.

* You can open the door for someone, but you can't walk through the doorway. In other words, do not invest a lot of time, energy, or attention into bullies. Keep your response short and simple. When bullies are ready to use their inner superhero instead of their inner villain, they will.

* Trust that life is growth! If I feel inner pain from something a bully said to me, I choose to look at this feeling as an opportunity to heal an insecurity within me. Just because someone noticed an opportunity for growth for you doesn't mean that makes you less of a human being. I internally or verbally thank the bully and say that I am not perfect. I thank the bully for showing me something I can focus on for growth! I choose to use my superhero decision making formula and how to deal worksheet. These will be explained later in this workbook.

* Don't give bullies the negative reaction they are looking for. Be positive, polite, and walk away.

* Putting yourself in a position of strength is choosing not to give your personal power (thoughts, attention, or behaviours) to bullies because you don't respect the behaviour. Power comes from accepting what happens. You can't change their behaviour - only they can. But

how you respond to their behaviour is key for not allowing bullies to affect you in any negative way.

Remember

The truth is when someone bullies it is not personal to you. Their reaction is a direct reflection of how they feel about themselves. Bullies are looking for a reaction from you; they are looking for more inner pain to feed their inner pain or inner villain. The truth is that bullies are lacking love in their lives, and so I will respond with love. I will give them what they are so desperately missing, even if they aren't aware of it. I will use my inner superhero to save me from the bully. Because of my inner superhero, when something really bothers me I know how to release that emotion in a healthy way. I know how to release my emotion in a way that frees and empowers myself and others through being the change I want to see in school and in life. You can do it too! You got this! Unleash your inner superhero today :) (More on the healthy releasing of emotions later in this book).

But what if you feel insecure about what a bully said?!
That is okay; it's time for growth! Allow me to share
some of my favourite healthy bully release activities!

Some of my favourite stress relievers are:

* journaling, writing out my personal story
* fitness activities like boxing and running
* talking with a friend, parent, or teacher
* meditation
* writing out my superpowers
* using my superhero decision making formula and how to deal work sheets
* baking
* painting or drawing
* finding something FUNNY to laugh about!

What activities can you engage in to release negative emotions?

HAVE FAITH YOU ARE NOT ALONE!

Birds of a Feather Flock Together

My negative inner villain behaviours increased
throughout grades 6, 7, and 8.

I began to hang out with kids who had similar pasts and experiences as a way to relate. It is predictable that kids who are brought up in abusive homes with broken families, addictions, and negative thinking tend to adopt these behaviours as well. Typically, these kids will naturally gravitate toward similar minds.

So it wasn't long until I started hanging out with the crowd who was daring enough to do the bad things that generally create addictions, pain, and suffering. This was the crowd that was skipping school, smoking, hanging out late at night, pushing boundaries, challenging authority, etc.

*Peer Pressure and Bullying started to Explode as
we began to compare ourselves to others.*

During these character building years, I was already feeling the effects of peer pressure. Influences were setting in. Everyone wanted to have the designer clothes and bags. As a girl, I felt the pressure of body image. I thought that my breasts had to be a certain size, my hair had to be a specific colour, my body type had to be a certain shape, my skin had to be flawless with make-up, etc. I remember sitting in class one day thinking I will be perfect and feel good about who I am when I have... fill in the blank. I had this mental checklist of materials I needed to feel worthy. I wanted specific clothes, hair, makeup, etc. I remember kids comparing themselves to each other and putting themselves down if they didn't have specific body sizes or designer clothes. I wasn't aware of it back then, but the school ground was full of insecure kids trying to find ways to make themselves feel good, important, worthy, and special, except that we were doing this in ways that caused harm onto others - and ultimately caused harm onto ourselves. When we cause harm to others, we are stripping away our own personal power and self esteem. People who behave like this have low levels of self confidence. Bullying doesn't work to create real, lasting self esteem and confidence because like an addiction, bullying needs to be refilled over and over again to experience the effects. Instead, why not work on ourselves to build REAL lasting confidence and self esteem - this is when others start to build up others - this is the ultimate feeling of power. This is our inner superhero at work!

I was aware of only one form of health.

As a young person, I was so involved in the physical world. I wasn't aware of what mental, emotional, and spiritual health was. I didn't realize or understand that every human being is special and important with their own unique talents, gifts, abilities, and skills that need to be celebrated. Back then I was mainly aware of the physical, materialistic, monetary world. Little did I know, sooner rather than later I was about to embark on the other levels of living that bring balance, joy, growth, peace, and success to life.

Reflecting on the years of Grades 6, 7, and 8

Looking back on those years; WOW... A lot happened and a lot went on. If I knew what I know now, I would have played those years differently. I would have used my words to express to my mom and dad how I felt. I would have participated in more sports and clubs to meet healthy friends. I wouldn't have allowed my parents' ordeal to affect my self-image and self esteem. I would have learned to speak up and not participate in bullying. This is why I am sooo excited to share with you the activities, challenges, and formulas I used to build the healthy self esteem, confidence, and mental health I needed to achieve goals and dreams. These techniques can give you the tools to power up and have a fabulous experience throughout school and life.

"Learning to overcome peer pressure, bullying, and negativity is a life skill. This is a life challenge/opportunity that doesn't

just exist during your school years but all throughout life. Life is growth; change is constant. Let's get good at it."

Grades 9 and 10

Allow me to share some stories from my high school years. These are the years my inner villain continued to develop and strengthen.

Oh, how I remember these days like they were yesterday. I was so nervous going into grade 9. It's normal to feel nervous going to a new environment with new people and expectations. To me, that shows you care.

High school brought on a lot of opportunities including sports teams, clubs, associations, a wide variety of classes, boys, and girls (new friendships and relationships) all while gearing up to decide what to do with our lives after graduation!

"Life is like a buffet: we can take what we want or we can leave it on the table. The choice is yours."

I saw these opportunities on the table, but I was fearful to try out for a school team or to try and make new friends. I didn't think people would like me. I was insecure about who I was because of the life events in my past. I was carrying around the family abuse and life events I had experienced while growing up inside of me.

"Later I learned we attract what we are."

I gravitated towards a crowd with a similar childhood story. Some of these kids were into committing crimes and doing drugs. It wasn't long until I began to start making those decisions as well. I was living with my dad with minimal supervision, and so I had a lot of freedom to do and say whatever I wanted.

"My life was like a snowball."

My life was one drama episode after another, and high school was the platform for more influences. I continued hanging out with the "bad" crowd and engaging in unhealthy behaviours. I was asked to smoke for the first time: I did it and hated it, but I kept smoking to fit in. I remember going to the bathroom to get sick, and then I came back out to smoke again. I didn't know this then, but my low self esteem and lack of confidence caused me to just follow the crowd. I remember something inside me didn't feel right, but I kept smoking anyways. I was not aware of why I was behaving like this. Things started to go downward and fast. Eventually that something inside me knew this was wrong and started to fade away to the point that I didn't feel it anymore.

Later I learned that something inside was my inner superhero...

Smoking cigarettes led to weed smoking and weed smoking led to harder drugs such as MDMA, cocaine, mushrooms, and prescription drugs. I began skipping school to smoke weed and lying to my dad about where I was going. The substances I was abusing led to enhanced levels of negativity such as depression, anxiety, low self worth, low self esteem, lack of self respect, etc. It wasn't long until I got in criminal trouble. I got suspended and expelled from the first high school I went to. I was arrested several times in grades 9 and 10. I think I went to five high schools. My poor decision making progressed pretty fast. My choices started to go deeper and deeper into serious trouble. I wasn't very aware of this, but my behaviour had changed. I began skipping more school. I was mean and rude to people by swearing, judging, and hating. I was an insecure bully. I was a selfish Drama Queen and everything was all about me. Oh, and I also knew everything on this planet; no one could tell me anything! My communication skills needed development. I didn't know how to communicate my feelings, and this caused me even more problems. My communication was outbursts of yelling and swearing. I allowed myself to be heavily influenced by the media, music, and movies... I began to not like who I was. I mean, who was this person I was becoming? Before I knew it, I was behaving similar to the lifestyle and life cycle that I had been born into. I was behaving like my upbringing but more intense.

School/Life Intervention

I was a troubled teen who needed guidance. I was wild and out of control. My inner villain was growing stronger. So my parents were brought together with the help of social workers and my school principal because I was getting into trouble. This was the first time in a long time I had seen my parents together and I was getting attention from them both. Even though it was bad attention, it was still attention and it was great to see them together.

But at this point in my life, I did not want to talk about the past. I was too far gone to want to help myself. My inner villain was very strong. My inner superhero was still there, but it was weak. I was not open minded. I was running away from myself in dealing with my "stuff". I was angry and blamed my parents and anyone else I could about their shortcomings without admitting my own. I was not ready to deal with my inner pain. My pain wanted to be left alone. Later I realized that ME, my inner superhero, needed to be there for Erica before anyone else could be.

I remember crying often during this time in my life. I was desperate for attention and love. All I wanted was to feel important, special, and worthy, but I was too scared to open up with myself or others. I didn't know how to be or how to live life. I was too scared to turn back to create a new beginning. I felt powerless. All this damage had been done and I now had this label about who I was and how I likely wouldn't change. There were many people who didn't believe in me. My family, my past elementary school friends, my family friends, and my acquaintances saw me differently now. I was scared and felt alone.

"No one believed in me, but most importantly I didn't believe in me to make a change."

I hit Rock Bottom.

Grades 9 and 10 were the years when I got in the most trouble. Allow me to break it down for you. I got suspended from school for fighting a girl, I was arrested for breaking into people's houses to steal, I stole from my parents, I lied all the time, I committed self-harm - I cut myself when I was high one night. I was so hurt and angry with everyone in the world, I began taking all kinds of drugs to soothe the pain. I was smoking weed often, which transitioned into doing drugs pretty much every day. At one point my dad took me to CAS centre to drop me off because he didn't know how to deal with me. That felt fun! I am obviously just kidding. That clearly hurt. My dad had asked me to come live with him, but when things got tough he wanted to throw me aside. He didn't want me to live with him anymore. My mom didn't want me to come live with her and her new boyfriend. So my dad thought that maybe the foster system would take me. I was arrested and sent to juvenile detention, and I was in and out and then back in again. There was a time when I got out of juvi and was back within 24 hours for stealing. Things got so bad that my dad finally kicked me out and I had nowhere to go. I did what some call "couch surfing" - not as fun as it sounds :) I was living with druggies which meant I wasn't living a clean life. I was partying all the time, staying out late, and sleeping all day.

"My inner superhero was searching."

I would call my mom every now and then. My mom would come searching for me all over the streets to rescue me, but I was in hiding. I didn't want to see my parents at this point. The only person that could rescue me was my inner superhero and I wasn't ready yet.

A traumatic Event that caused severe inner pain

One day I experienced a life event that took me a long time to overcome - I was raped. I was 15 years old when this happened. I was hanging out with a crowd that was doing bad things already. When this happened I was in lots of pain: physically, mentally, emotionally, and spirituality. I remember this event like yesterday. I got myself out of the situation and ran home. I went to the hospital with my mom to make sure everything was okay, but I didn't report what happened and didn't let my mom know. I was embarrassed and ashamed to talk about it. The truth of the matter is that I lost my virginity through rape. This was not how I had envisioned it would happen. I didn't know this then, but this experience affected my relationship with men for many years to come. It wasn't until the awakening of my inner superhero that I released the past pain and was able to attract healthy male relationships - more on this later. At that time in my life, I felt so abused, fearful, and stressful. Up until the awakening I was searching for answers. I was searching for the truth of why the past events happened and how to work through the pain so it didn't consume me anymore.

A decision to last a lifetime - THANK YOU MAMA!

The last time that I was in custody, I was 15 years old, and I was given the choice to go to a group home or back home with my dad. It would have been so easy to go back home with my dad - no rules, no structure, no tough love. I basically got to do what I wanted, when I wanted, and how I wanted, but at the end of all that I wasn't happy. I was looking for direction and guidance to live a good life, and I had to be honest with myself. I was depressed and life had presented me with an opportunity. I spoke to my mom about my decision. I have to give credit here to my mama who influenced me to make the choice that was aligned with my best interest for healthy living. My mom said that the group home would give me a chance to make a good life. I was on the fence, and a big part of me didn't want to go.

I mean, a group home didn't sound that appealing compared to the situation I had before in terms of freedom, but I knew I needed change. Looking back now, what was holding me back was a matter of power and control. I knew that in the group home I wouldn't have the same freedom that I would have living at home, but in the group home there was so much more life education, attention, care, and tough love! I had to stand up for me and fight to get my life back on track.

The scales were outweighed. My pain had more power over my decision making. I had to learn how to build up my positive, light, and loving side - a.k.a. my inner superhero...

Something to Think About...

As I said, a big part of me didn't want to go, but there was a part inside of me that said yes (later I found out that was my inner superhero).

Choosing to live in the group home was a building block of awakening my Inner Superhero.

I was taking an action that would build up my inner superhero, my positivity, and my personal power. I basically started doing the opposite of everything I had been doing before. I was going to school. I was clean from smoking, drinking, and drugs. I kept my promises. I was feeding myself good healthy foods, working out, etc. I was feeding my inner superhero.

"I began strengthening and powering UP my inner superhero."

So I went to go live in the group home. I remember having a hard time looking at myself in the mirror, wondering how I got to this point in my life. I decided right then and there to give myself a shot to be healthy and happy. I was committed to turning my life around. I wanted to laugh again. I wanted to feel happy. After all, deep down inside of me, I wanted to live a healthy happy life. I wanted to feel good without being dependent on any substance or anyone. I wanted freedom and inner peace in my life. ***My inner superhero was on the path of emerging.***

My Journey to Self Discovery

I was addicted to drugs and had recently experienced withdrawal while in custody. I needed to go to a program to discover why I was engaging in these behaviours of using substances. The group home had access to other programs that had access to funding to attend a recovery program. I attended a 30-day recovery program in Thunder Bay Ontario where I had the opportunity to focus just on me, my health, and the pieces I felt were missing. I quit smoking, got clean, and focused on activities that brought me joy like yoga, fitness, and spirituality. Parts of the real Erica were emerging (my inner superhero).

Ask and You Shall Receive

I learned to ask for forgiveness and work through my own pain. I learned to ask for my needs to be fulfilled. I began to focus on positive affirmations through prayer to guide me through life challenges and to achieve life dreams. Asking for guidance opened up doors to receive the answers.

I WAS BUILDING MY PERSONAL POWER.

When I returned from Thunder Bay I was going into Grade 11. I was enthusiastic to get my life in order. I was looking forward to going back to school to give myself the chance and opportunity to succeed like I never had before! From the inspiration of a staff mentor, I started a Social Justice and Peace Club. I wanted to give back to the community for what I felt I had taken away. This staff mentor has been one of the most profound relationships in my life. Not only did he inspire me to live a healthy lifestyle, get my life in order, create a social justice group, and empower myself through serving others, but he was the first male relationship I had that was healthy. He taught me what a healthy male and female friendship was. I still talk to him today. In fact, his mom is the person who introduced me to public speaking. I am ever so grateful to have lived in the group home and connected with these wonderful human beings!

My Second Chance at Succeeding in High School

As I said, the group home opened doors for me. I got a second chance to succeed in school and that is what I did. I began attending classes, engaging in homework, and building relationships with peers and teachers. In Grade 11, I really started to shift my thinking and behaviour. I took an Exercise Science class that inspired me to begin teaching fitness. In my early years in elementary school, I had always been athletic by thriving in school track and field meets. I had a passion for sports and athletics. So when I had the choice to write an essay or design and teach a fitness class to all the students, well, let's just say it was a no brainer. I began watching TY-BO DVDs, working out at the gym, and taking fitness classes. I felt so ALIVE! This is when I began to fall in love with fitness. I taught the fitness class and aced it. I discovered that I absolutely loved teaching others about fitness. So naturally, when we reached the point in high school of thinking about what to do next, I began searching for careers in the fitness industry. I learned what it took to become a Personal Trainer and began the certification journey. I've been teaching health and fitness ever since.

"I found that Fitness was one of MY SUPERHERO SUPERPOWERS. I was BUILDING MY INNER STRENGTH because it felt so good to work out. Fitness gave me a natural high, and throughout the process of working out I built self esteem, confidence, and inner strength."

FITNESS BECAME THE LOVE OF MY LIFE!

I got a membership at the YMCA and engaged in a variety of types of fitness activities. I was focusing on a balanced approach to the health and wellbeing of my mind, heart, soul, and body. I took courses and studied cardiovascular, strength, and flexibility training to implement into my life. I was feeding my inner superhero positivity and health which resulted in my happiness.

I have so much respect for group homes! Thank you, life!

I cannot imagine my life without living in the group home today. Living in the group home brought on many opportunities and resources which I may otherwise not have been able to experience. I experienced the structure, life skills, accountability, discipline, health care, mentorship, coaching, and friendship that I needed to heal through the addictions, abuse, and negative mindset and create a lifestyle that I desired. Little did I know then, but I was embarking on a journey of self discovery that would open many doors for me.

After living in the group home for a year, I moved out on my own with a roommate - a fantastic gal who I met through working at a local convention centre. She was fabulous. I lived with her until I moved on to College.

When I was in College I started working for a company that allowed students to make money around their course schedule. This company gave students the opportunity to run their own summer business in between school years. I pursued this company and was elected to become a Branch Manager. At this point I independently opened up shop in Cambridge, Ontario. I interviewed, hired, and trained sales professionals to sell a wonderful line of cutlery. This was an AMAZING business experience as I learned business skills including how to recruit, coach, retain, develop, and speak publicly. I developed leadership skills and was strengthening my inner superhero by serving others and my community.

But I was stuck in unhealthy relationship patterns.

During this time I met a guy who I eventually decided to live with. Long story short, it was an unhealthy relationship. Remember how I said I had adopted my family's unhealthy relationship habits? This was the deepest unhealthy relationship I had been in. I was unaware and as a result I was verbally, emotionally, and financially abused by this person because I still wasn't fully awake or aware of my behaviours with others. I didn't see the warning signs before going into this relationship, and we broke up while I was still living in his house. I felt like I was failing in life. I felt lost, confused, lonely, and depressed and didn't see a way out of the pain I was experiencing.

I tried to end my life.

MY DEEPEST DESIRE

All I wanted was to connect with someone. I wanted to feel supported and important. I wanted to receive attention and love. I wanted to feel a connection with others...

My self-image and self esteem decreased, becoming lower and lower. I felt powerless over what was happening around me. I still didn't realize that I had personal power. My mind didn't know personal power existed.

I felt depressed.

I felt in such a low place, it was like negative energy was consuming me. My thought processes were unhealthy. I was taking prescription drugs, drinking, and staying home from work because it felt so hard to just be alive. I felt like it was the only way out - this was to end my life. This was a cry out for help. I felt powerless and trapped. I couldn't see solutions and I feel so emotionally bruised and hurt. My inner villain was consuming me. My inner superhero didn't want to die, but I didn't know how to deal with life's challenges. My inner superhero was there but had little power.

"What I didn't know was there was still unresolved pain and unfinished business from my past that I hadn't dealt with. This pain was coming out through a relationship."

I had massive amounts of pain to deal that would take time to clear. This pain came in waves. Looking back now, what I know for sure is that you have to be ready to face your pain. I recommend taking the time you need to facilitate long-term healing and use the resources available to you like prayer, school, family support, etc.

Healing is a process which takes time.

I was moving forward in life and sometimes taking a couple of steps back. I still carried some fear and I still embodied negativity. I would experience waves of depression and anxiety. I would look for relationships to fill the hole I felt inside.

After the suicide attempt I realized I had been looking for people and for things outside of me to solve my problems. In this situation I had looked for a boy to solve my problems. I had given past events personal power because I had allowed the past events to define me. I had adapted to their identity and lifestyle and forgot my own. I did not have an opinion. I had looked for someone else to make me happy.

As a result, I was unhappy. I didn't realize that happiness came from within.

My purpose is to change the stigma of suicide.

I am here to tell the world that people who are suicidal are at the verge of a breakthrough. If this is you or someone you know, then I encourage you to tell them. The truth of the matter is that the pain they are feeling within is real to them. They are reaching the point of either releasing the pain and letting go, or else letting the pain consume their life.

I believe that my inner superhero awakened to let go and release the inner pain I was holding onto. You see, I was resisting and wanting to change what had happened in the past. Once I accepted what had happened and realized I had no power to change the past, I understood that the power I have is to make different decisions and to look at situations differently. My superpower was to see the life lessons. I discovered this through a desperate way to be healthy. I promise it will happen! You've got to fight hard to strengthen your inner superhero to save you from your inner villain. This is an internal war worth fighting for. You are naturally designed and have the power to do this! YOU'VE GOT the POWER!

I am persistent, forgiving, loving, and happy to be alive!

A part of trusting the natural process of life is knowing that as human beings we are naturally designed and created to know how to release our inner pain. Life truly has a way of guiding us to release and let go of our inner pain. You are guided to live a healthy and happy life, no matter what family you are born into, where you live, or what events have happened in your life.

A YEAR LATER...

MY INNER SUPERHERO
WOKE UP!

THE AWAKENING OF MY INNER SUPERHERO

When I was 21 I experienced an awakening that completely changed my life. I woke up my own inner superhero. A part of waking up was realizing that I had this power all along. With this personal power which I call my superpower, I was able to overcome hard emotions such as suicidal thoughts, depression, and anxiety and begin enhancing the feelings of self esteem, self love, and confidence that would lead me to my own recovery and success in life and business. I began to embrace my inner superhero. I realized that all my activities, choices, decisions, and actions of the past had led to this wakeup call! BAM!

I often get asked about what it felt like. It felt like being born for the first time - spiritually speaking. Some Christians explain that this is like a rebirth. An awakening process is like being born for the first time!

I felt like I was looking at life for the first time.

I would love nothing more than to share with you my experience of what happened when I woke up. Again, this process SAVED MY LIFE!!! My inner superhero emerged.

I remember this experience like it was yesterday; I remember it vividly. I had just gotten back from a work conference entitled "The Time is Now". I truly believe that this verbiage and theme of the conference planted a seed that later came to fruition in my awakening. I share this piece with you because I believe life has a way of showing us "signs". We receive messages from people, events, and objects that we can choose to assign meaning to in order to guide our life growth.

My awakening came to be through unresolved anger from my past. When I got back from the conference I felt like I needed to communicate my feelings of hurt and anger to a friend.

When I was communicating my frustrations, I looked at my friend and I could see that he was in so much pain - I realized that the words I was saying were causing him pain. This realization froze me as I could see his pain. It was in that moment that he said to me... "Erica, close your eyes." I remember I was sooo afraid.... My friend had to tell me seven times to close my eyes before I actually did. I remember feeling SOOO much fear. I had never felt that much fear in my life. When I closed my eyes, my friend walked me through a meditation exercise where I connected with my inner child. He guided me through exercises to connect with inner Erica. I was to BE with HER and comfort her. It was THEN when I realized that I had connected with ME - my inner superhero.

I consciously connected with my Inner Superhero for the first time.

He was my mirror where for the first time I saw for real that my pain was causing pain onto others. My friend's pain had reflected my inner pain. Throughout our experience and relationship, our time together showed me that I had unresolved negative emotions.

I EXPERIENCED THE PRESENT MOMENT FOR THE FIRST TIME.

What is the present moment? It is pure love; pure love that radiates to everyone around you and throughout the world. The present moment is non-judgmental and accepts things and people for what and who they are. When I woke up, I was completely submerged in the present moment. This is when I became HIGH on life. Every addict's dream! I remember being. Yes, BEING. I learned what it was like to step into alignment with love and step out of my way of fear. This was the ultimate feeling of freedom! There is no past living within you or future determined for you. You are completely present in the moment. I was in complete and total bliss, at ease and present.

Before I woke up I had been experiencing serious depression and anxiety. Depression is experiencing past pain or trauma over and over again, and anxiety is fear of the future.

When I woke up I realized that I had the power all along. I realized that it was me who needed the guidance. All the attention, love, and care was something that I could give to myself.

I BECAME HIGH ON LIFE.

At this point in my journey I began to fall in love with life and me. I began to love everything life had to offer. I loved the trees, sky, animals, cars, and people. All was well and heavenly. It felt like heaven on earth. It didn't matter how much money I had or what type of car I drove. I was so in love with the state of being. This is when I developed my personal definition of success:

Erica's definition of success:

"Living a healthy and happy life with love, treating myself and other people well, while living up to my life's purpose, doing my life's work, and sharing the journey with others."

I began to realize that I was not alone!

Do you know there are over 196 countries on this planet, with over seven billion human inhabitants? There are many, many, many experiences to be had. Think about the possibilities. I started to realize that everyone has their own pains, hurts, growth opportunities, success, etc. I started to realize that everyone has their life journey and life purpose.

NO MATTER WHAT HAPPENED IN MY LIFE, I
REALIZED I COULD CREATE MY OWN LIFESTYLE
AND LIFECYCLE TO BUILD THE LIFE I WANT.

WE ARE ALL BORN INTO A LIFE CYCLE. SOMETIMES WE NEED TO UNLEARN TO RELEARN.

I now understood that my parents had passed down a life cycle that had been passed down onto them by their own parents without ever consciously asking: "Is this the life cycle that I want to implement in my life and pass down to my kids?" In my opinion, life cycles have the intention to shift and grow. For example, my dad passed down his ideas and thoughts that this world is evil, not to trust anyone, and that life is hard and a struggle. My mom unconsciously passed down her view that only certain men will want me, men who would tolerate my shortcomings.

If I were to adopt these beliefs, then I would be living a completely different life than I am today. Something inside me that I later discovered was my inner superhero told me that these beliefs were not me. I comprehended that I didn't have to adopt these beliefs - that I had a choice. I later realized that these beliefs were derived from the misconceptions of society and from my own parents' insecurities. I remember living my life in fear. God bless my parents. I forgive them! They were not awake or aware. I know they did the best they could with the knowledge and resources they had!

The AH-HA MOMENT

When I woke up my inner superhero, I realized the truth: I can create my own life cycle because I am the creator of my own life. So that is what I did.

I CREATED MY OWN LIFE CYCLE.

I created my own curriculum for success. I studied psychology and sociology in college; attended workshops on real estate, personal empowerment, sales, health, and wellbeing; went to fitness classes, etc. Like a clean slate, I had to acquire the knowledge and skills to create the life of my dreams - on my own. I knew that no one else on this planet could give me what I desired within but me. I had to step up. Have you heard the saying that when the student is ready the teacher will appear? I asked for guidance through prayer, and guess what I received? The answers. This technique worked because of the power I give the activities I engage in. I put trust and faith into my personal growth work.. With the key ingredients of a deep burning desire to experience a life change and commitment to doing whatever it takes, I experienced success. I started to realize that the answers, people, and opportunities always appeared in divine time and order - exactly when I was ready for them.

After my awakening I was truly ready to do whatever it took to achieve my goals and dreams. That meant a deep commitment. I was being completely honest with myself.

Habit is a Strong Force.

I had spent a large part of my life focusing on the negative, dwelling on the past, and reflecting on what I felt others had done to me. I was in perpetual victim mode, but I wasn't seeing the truth. I wasn't seeing reality. I had created my own reality that was creating fear. It was like a never ending bad movie that was playing over and over again. When I ignited my inner superhero, it was like feeling free for the first time. I was completely in the present moment. I was free of fear, judgments, criticisms, worry, anger, stress, and any other uncomfortable feeling of pain.

When I woke up my inner superhero I started to see life differently. I understood that what had happened to me in the past was simply just that - the past. I realized that I got to choose who I am. I realized that I got to choose whether or not to allow my past to define me. I realized that every moment was a new moment in time and that no matter what happened in my life, I could be who I wanted to be.

I could define my own character. I began to see people differently. I began to forgive people who had physically, mentally, sexually, emotionally, and spiritually hurt me. I forgave my abusers through seeing the truth: they were only being that way because they themselves had been mistreated and abused. They were simply passing on their abuse. I began to take things not so personally because I realized it was never about me - it was all about them. I cannot control what goes on in the world or what life events occur in my life that impact me directly or indirectly, but I can certainly control how I respond to them and that is where our power lies. That is the power of our inner superhero. I have it, and you have it too. It is time for you to realize your full inner power and claim what is rightfully yours.

Remember Life Loves You!

When I woke up to my inner superhero I woke up to the truth. The truth is that life loves you and love is available to you in various forms of living. My goal for you is to develop a strong relationship with life. Learn to move with its cycles and currents, develop strong resilient muscles, and see challenges and obstacles as growth opportunities. Learn how to exercise your own personal power through your thoughts and actions; these ultimately bring about the results you are looking for in life. The truth is that we are born for a purpose and the creator loves us. You are so loved! We have the power of choice. We have the power to choose how to think, what to think, what to say to others, and what to say to ourselves. Change your thoughts and you will change your life. This is the biggest and best gift of life you can receive.

I gave myself permission to move forward fearlessly!

You've got to give yourself permission to go out there and receive what you want in life, whether it is being your own hero, being your own best friend, being your own parent, or being your own boss. I think you get the point :)

When I woke up, my inner superhero pushed through the fear which saved my life. This process has led to the most rewarding and best experiences in my life!

Waking up your inner superhero is a process and takes time!

This was the beginning of a transformation process that still continues today! You see I had lived for 21 years of my life with my inner villain having more power. So it was going to take time to continue to build and power up my inner superhero. Because I hadn't been aware of my decisions for so long, I had been making decisions out of a place of pain without realizing it.

There have been times of misunderstanding for myself and others.

There have been times of feeling misunderstood because my inner superhero wasn't making my decisions, but the presence was NOW there and awake! It felt like my inner superhero had been watching my inner villain make these choices: some call this the witnessor. My inner superhero had been so patient with my inner villain, and now my inner superhero had influence over my inner villain. After my awakening, often I communicated words that I knew weren't aligned with my inner superhero simply out of habit. But then I would correct myself right away because I know words have power, and I know the power of conditioning.

There have been times when my inner villain resisted my inner superhero. After a few days of pure bliss, I went back into old habits. My inner superhero had to keep working with my inner villain to gain more power and guide me toward healthy living. I stayed focused, was patient, and emphasized the small and big wins. I knew that if I kept my eye on the prize that one day my inner superhero would be FULLY powered!

This is an ongoing practice that have persevered through well. Today my inner superhero has more power due to practice and persistence. This process have been one of the most incredible processes in my life!

I am so excited that when I choose to create a family I will pass on teachings, attitudes, and behaviours of the inner superhero to my kids so that they can go create another superhero life cycle! I want to pass on my greatness to my children so that they can live the most healthy, happy, loving, and successful lives!

My inner superhero found love for my inner villain. This led to my wakeup call!

Erica's activities that facilitated awakening her inner superhero

The truth is that every individual has their own experience and steps that will facilitate their awakening. Remember, you have the power within to guide yourself through to discovery. You will uncover the steps to attracting the people and opportunities that will give you the answers to get you there.

Remember, you are naturally designed to work together as one to create the life you desire. Learn to trust yourself and life. Have you heard the quote: "Life is simple; as human beings we tend to complicate things"? This is so true! Let's keep our life simple.

Here is a guideline of activities I highly recommend to engage in to enhance the self esteem, confidence, personal power, and love within you. These activities will help you to live and create a great life. These were my activities that I engaged in to facilitate awakening my inner superhero. I challenge you to have your own experience. This is why I am giving you the activities without all my answers. I DARE you to do them!

1. Three-Day Silence Exercise
   This three-day silence exercise is exactly what it sounds like. Pick three days and practice silent meditation. I've done this exercise twice. When I planned this exercise I picked two holidays where I had three days off in a row. I let my family know that I was doing this. Some were supportive and some were not. I did it anyways.

2. Schedule a date night designed for you!
   I scheduled a date night for me where I cooked my favourite foods and watched some of my favourite movies. This activity teaches you to learn how to be comfortable being alone and comfortable in your own skin and practice being happy alone.

3. Declutter and clean your environments.
   Clean your closet, your room, the house, etc. Clean any place that is yours. Clean up your emails and social media accounts. Ensure that you only have people and objects in your life that are positive and healthy for your lifestyle. I recommend repeating this process whenever you feel the need to. I declutter approximately once every three months, or as I said - whenever I feel the need to. I donate clothing and furniture that I no longer use or need. One of my girlfriends

loves to do this with me. She loves decluttering. Invite anyone in the process with you or do it on your own. At the end, I usually feel as if weight has been lifted off my shoulders. You will feel AMAZING!!!

4. Give back to others.
   I love giving back to others because it feels good. When I give to others I am giving to myself. I give to others in various ways. I give sincere, genuine compliments, and I focus on the positive of what people say. If I hear a friend or acquaintance mention something negative about their body image, I focus on finding something positive to say to them. We are all beautiful in our own way. I buy tea or coffee for my friends or I will pay for the person behind me in a drive-thru. I love to volunteer my time with people who need a boost of love or confidence in their lives. I volunteer at places such as shelters, Big Sisters, juvenile centres, etc. It feels so good. Interestingly enough, opportunities and doors have opened from volunteering which was a nice byproduct of doing what I loved to do anyways. I find that life has a way of supporting you as you take positive steps in your life and in the lives of others.

5. Acceptance
   This was big one for me. Accept life, people, and life events for who and what they are. Once I learned that the power is not trying to control what has happened or is happening, but rather in how I respond to the situation - I immediately enhanced my confidence and trust for life. True power comes from accepting past life events and learning from them.

6. Keep a Journal.
   I love journaling and writing. Writing has been a healing instrument for me to let go of my emotions and express my feelings in a healthy way. I think I have kept over 10 journals

in my lifetime. I challenge you to write in a journal. Write anything you want to write about. I recommend that you get a journal that you LOVE... Chapters and Dollarama have fantastic journals. The best journals to buy are the ones that you use most often! Make it your own. Make it personalized so that you enjoy the process and use it often.

7. Eat healthily and work out regularly.
   Food gives you energy and it takes a lot of energy to build self esteem, confidence, and positivity into our lives. Focus on foods your body loves and enjoys! Fitness fuels the body and it feels so good!

8. Behave like the world is watching you. Be proud of where you have come from through celebrating failures and success. Having a strong accountability system is key to enhancing your awesomeness and love.

9. Recognize that our inner superhero is a presence and there is a great force behind that force. This force is greater than your emotions and thoughts. Focus on that force and energy, as it will guide you to make healthy and happy decisions.

10. Have Faith and Trust in the natural processes of life. Having a strong faith in life while knowing that we are resilient human beings who can bounce back from anything is powerful.

11. Believe in the Power of Nature and Meditation.
    I began to be curious about exploring and engaging in new experiences. I naturally began to want to spend time outside. I love nature. Nature has a comforting way about her. I love the fresh air and how comfortable I feel being outside. Spending time in nature allowed time for me and my mental health. I would clear my head and practice focusing my thoughts

on positivity. If something or someone was bothering me, I would go outside and meditate. I began focusing my thoughts on the direction of where I wanted to go in life.

12. Don't Give Up - Persistence Pays Off! Life has a way of developing us to become stronger and independent. Have faith and keep moving forward until you reach your desired goal! Sometimes you've got to fight hard until you reach that goal!

What I recommend for parents

WOW! We just went through a lot!

In my personal experience, I have been teaching my parents the power of the inner superhero. This has been and continues to be an honour! Through sharing stories, spending time together, being the person I want others to be, and communicating I have shown my parents how to tap into their inner superhero!

For those parents out there, if your child is going through something similar to what I went through in my school years, I suggest that you apply these techniques. I promise it will make a difference!

1. Give unconditional love and undivided attention while setting healthy boundaries.
2. Do activities together by spending time with your child.
   At the end of the day, your child has to be ready to make a change. You can do everything within your power, but if your child is not ready, then he is not ready. When your child is ready, then he will change. Trust life and have faith. Someone once told me this about parenting: "It will be all right in the end. And if it's not all right, then it's not the end."
   I think of these words often.
3. Trust life and timing! Life has a plan for you and your child. Some challenges come up in our life often to build strength and prepare us for something great in the future! Putting trust out to the world and life will attract good experiences for you and your child.
4. Live your best life by living by example! Be the change you want to see! I know this can be challenging at times, but it works! Keep doing this until you get results! Trust that your child has their own life purpose, free will, and choice.

Let go and believe in them. Focus on the inner superhero and greatness. LOVE heals all wounds. When in doubt, show unconditional love!

5. Find the positives because it just feels good!

Notes:____

MY PASSION TO WAKE UP OTHER SUPERHEROES

My Superpowers Were Released to Awaken Other Superheroes

Once I learned how to awaken my inner superhero, I had a deep burning desire to work with others. I wanted to teach others how to release their own inner superhero. The platform where I naturally knew how to do this was in the fitness world. I am going to explain to you some valuable life lessons I learned upon awakening my inner superhero and applying them to my professional life.

In this section, I will share my professional fitness journey, client success stories, training philosophy, and client approach that has led to the success stories of thousands of others.

When I experienced my inner superhero awakening, my life began to change very fast. I felt passionate about using my superpowers **(natural talents, gifts, abilities, and skills)** to inspire others. I wanted to teach others how to find their inner superhero to achieve their own fitness goals and dreams. My heart and soul are invested in fitness. I had fallen in love with the countless benefits of fitness! I LOVE the natural feel good "high" - (Fitness became my drug!) I loved how being fit enabled me to focus on building strength and health - and I could fit into my clothes better. I was able to release and channel any negative emotions in a healthy way. Fitness was my channel - my vehicle to share my passion with others.

I hold nine Fitness/Health Certifications.

I began taking course after course educating myself on psychology, physiology, nutrition, meditation, life coaching, exercise science, and more. As of today, I currently hold nine fitness and health certifications through Canada's Largest Fitness Network. With the combination of my knowledge, passion, and deep burning desire for purpose I began the hunt to serve others.

I was building business skills.

I became the #1 Fitness Instructor in the Country for Canada's Largest Fitness BootCamp!

One of my girlfriends referred me to work at Canada's Largest Fitness Camp Company. So I applied, met with the CEO, and got hired. The position functioned like a Franchisee Model. I owned a territory and the company split marketing/business costs to build the business. I took over a territory that was struggling with low attendance. So coming into the business I had to boost sales - and fast - to profit my time, energy, and efforts. After a few months of action I was on my way to success.

This was a women's only fitness class for all ages and all fitness levels. The classes I ran were so popular that I sold out consistently. I reached thousands of people through what people called the Erica Effect. Every four weeks we would run fitness assessments as a checkpoint to measure results. I didn't like how women beat themselves up at the fitness measurement, and so I adopted a new form of success measurement. Through Fitness Tests, I customized and tailored the monthly fitness assessments to the group's needs. This way the ladies were able to see how much growth they had experienced in the areas of strength, power, flexibility, eating habits, and more. I created goal sheets so that they could focus their goals around mental, emotional, and spiritual health - the big picture of health. My ladies were seeing amazing results quickly! Not to mention I was setting them up for long-term success through personal empowerment, monthly success check-ins, long-term lifestyle changes, and inspiring growth in their relationships through working out with others in their life and community events.

My fitness classes were like motivational speaking classes. I used inspiring words to motivate movement with the participants and focus on reaching their inner superhero. I applied my superpowers which were the power of positive words, energy, passion for fitness, and understanding the power of multiple fitness health levels (mental, emotional, and spiritual) to facilitate physical movement and behaviour in the lives of others. Not only was I inspiring physical workouts to promote healthy living, but I was reaching clients' minds, hearts, and souls. As a result, they were positively impacting their bodies. I taught them how to empower themselves to develop their own personal power within. This way, clients could learn to be resilient and empower themselves to achieve not only their fitness goals but any life goal.

To enhance the client experience and build morale, I implemented Ladies' Night after every eight-week program - to celebrate success, have fun, laugh, and connect on a deeper level. The community that was created was strong.

The Game Changer for Clients

Throughout my professional studies and personal experiences, I began to connect the dots on what it took to achieve a healthy lifestyle change. I began to understand how to set people up for success long after our time together was done. Clients typically came to me because they were searching for a physical difference; however, the core of what they were looking for was so much more. The truth of the matter is that human beings crave health on multiple levels of living (physical, mental, emotional, spiritual, and relational health). I quickly learned that teaching fitness was not only for the physical benefits; teaching fitness was actually the vehicle to reach clients' pain spots.

The truth is our physical health is only one piece of the puzzle to living a healthy, fulfilled, loving life. Some of these levels are often missed which results in plateaus, decreased results, and failures.

Sometimes we need to reset, rebuild, and refocus.

There are building blocks to building and creating your life full of love, health, and happiness. Sometimes we need to wipe the slate clean and start new - like painting on a blank canvas. We need to select the proper equipment including paintbrushes and paints; select the right teacher; and attend the right classes. We must then guide ourselves through applying the techniques and tools. When I train, coach, and speak, I constantly convey that the audience members have the power. They are choosing to allow my truths, teaching, and stories to positively impact them or not. It is my ultimate mission for the audience to know how to empower themselves. My passion is so large here, because I want clients to achieve long-term success even after I am gone. I want clients to apply what they have learned with me and feel empowered to apply their new learning to all areas of their lives. This mindset results in higher success. They are enhancing their own independent thinking and behaviour. Ultimately, they will have gathered the tools to paint a beautiful masterpiece of their life.

Clients' Goals Were More Than Physical

Some wanted to lose weight, build muscle, increase energy, and be proactive towards unhealthily genetics. I know fitness was the main attraction to achieving health, but there was more below the surface. Some ladies were looking for more than they were aware of in their pursuit of health. *At the end of the day, I found clients were looking for connection, a strong sense of self, a sense of purpose, and establishing a clear vision of a healthy body - mentally, emotionally, and spiritually.* To promote independence, clients were responsible for committing to workouts outside of our classes to build a healthy lifestyle and reach their goals.

Read some stories from my amazing fitness clients!

"I'm so thankful to have my amazing trainer Erica, who keeps the energy up, keeps me motivated, and changes the routine every class. I have seen physical benefits, but the mental benefits have been outstanding! My mood and energy levels have increased exponentially. I feel like a new person, becoming more confident and outgoing. I can perform more tasks in my daily life, that I had difficulty prior to camp. I am proud of myself and so are my family and friends, for making these essential changes in my life and sticking to them. I'm so motivated to continue

this new healthy lifestyle, that I signed up for another 8 week session."
Miranda

"Working out with Erica leading our group of ladies was so inspiring and so much fun, I look forward to meeting with them every week! I joined to help myself gain a positive attitude towards my health and exercise and it definitely delivered. I left happy, motivated, and happy with my body the way it is. Erica really went the extra mile to help me think strong, not just skinny. I recommend working with Erica to anyone."
Lindsay N.

"I've learned when you help others reach their goals you will naturally achieve your goals."

-Erica

My dedication, passion, and application of my superpowers brought so much success for these ladies. I worked with over 1000 ladies to guide them along their health and fitness journeys. As a result, I was awarded the highest level of achievement within the company. I was awarded for number of sales in helping the most people achieve their fitness and health goals. I was awarded a fabulous trip to Bali, Indonesia for a surf goddess retreat. I was sooo excited and couldn't wait to go. I was the first person in my family to travel to the southwest hemisphere. I was so grateful to win this award. My success came from helping other people succeed and it was so much fun!

"Empowering others led to others empowering themselves and their inner superheroes."

Working with these amazing ladies inspired some of them to want to pursue careers in fitness as well. I was so proud of their work and their stories were so inspirational. Some overcame depression, anxiety, and mood changes. Through waking up their inner superhero they felt more energized, happy, healthy, and comfortable in their skin all by living the day-to-day more healthily.

When I got into speaking I couldn't help but share my burning passion for fitness. I wanted to find a FUN way to engage students on all levels. This was when Fitness Concerts were born.

How Fitness Concerts were created!

Maybe you've taken one of my fitness concert classes or seen one of my videos. I created fitness concerts to connect with students by creating a FUN way to exercise together.

Fitness Concerts = UPBEAT FUN Music + Fitness + Motivational Speaking

I love working out with students of all ages. I love sharing the healthy components of workout and the POWER of fitness activities such as yoga, meditation, strength training, cardio, and most importantly how to make these activities FUN! Let's be honest: the more fun our workouts are the more likely we will be consistent with them.

"Erica's fitness concerts were super fun and a great workout. She makes fitness fun!"

-Student CAS

Students' Success Stories

"YOU'RE BEAUTIFUL! The grade 10 girls from St. Andre are sending these high fives and sunshine to you every day. I believe we all needed the reminders and hope you instilled within us. You were a gallon of sparkles and sunshine which was so refreshing. I'm sure you hear it a lot, but you deserve to hear that you're inspiring. What you do is inspiring and who YOU are is inspiring! Thank you, Thank you, Thank you!"

Lots of love to a beautiful woman from your beautiful grade 10 Saint Andre Bessette girls.

"The most valuable part to our girls' day was when the guest speaker made us realize that we all are beautiful and strong to overcome life's challenges."

Student from St. Andre Bessette

"The guest speaker was most valuable to me because she was very informative and connected with us. We loved her workouts."

Student from St Mary's High School

You see personal growth has been an agent of change for myself and others. Taking action has created life! You can hear the best stories, techniques and programs in the world, but if nothing has been applied then nothing will change. This is why the rest of the book is a workbook.

Part 2: How to POWER UP your Inner Superhero

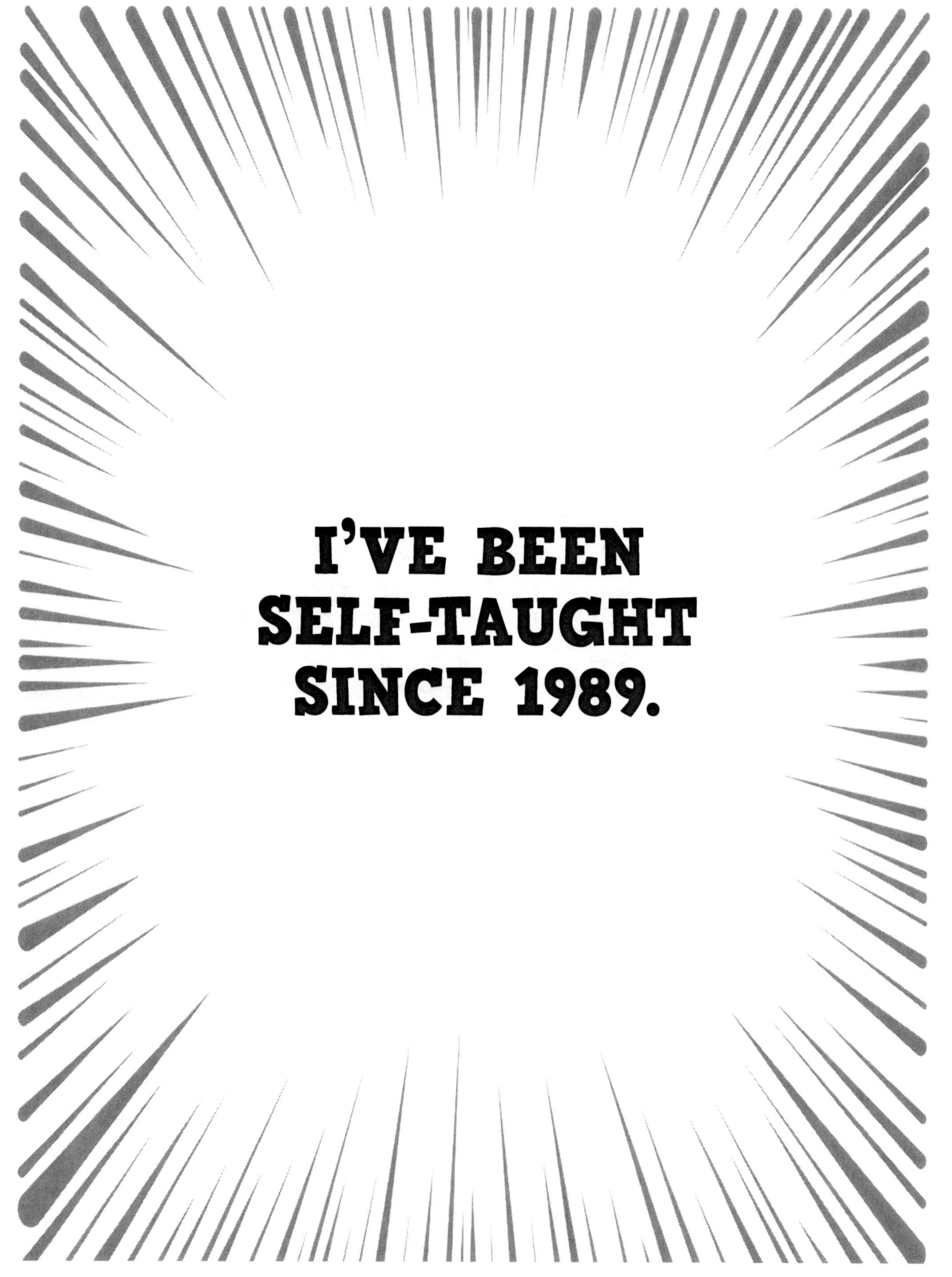
I'VE BEEN
SELF-TAUGHT
SINCE 1989.

Let's Build Your Inner Superhero Together

Alright, I've talked a lot about your inner superhero. It is time to step into how to awaken or enhance the awakening of your inner superhero to live the life of your dreams! Are you ready?

In this section, I am going to share with you stories, activities, formulas, and growth challenges that will guide you to focus on developing your inner superhero. I am going to share with you how I overcame negative thinking and low energy emotions like anxiety and depression. I am going to tell you how I raised these energy vibrations through building self esteem, confidence, and personal power which ultimately led to waking up my inner superhero.

I will highlight how I've achieved my goals and dreams such as graduating high school, achieving nine fitness and health certifications, earning award-winning results within a fitness company, taking courses in psychology and sociology in college, traveling the world, and developing strong intrapersonal and interpersonal relationships with myself, family, friends, professionals, and community that have brought me so much happiness, health, and success. I am sharing with you the activities I have used and still use today to navigate through life's challenges and achieve my life's dreams.

Are you ready to follow along in this workbook to produce your inner superhero?

There are four components to building your inner superhero and they must be followed in a specific order.

Note: It is recommended to work through these activities in a certain order so that the success of each building block will build on one another. However, this doesn't mean that you won't go back and forth between sections as sometimes you will shift between success within the four building blocks. My hope is that you remain open and flexible to achieve your desired goals and trust your inner superhero to guide you.

Building Blocks to awakening your inner superhero:

1. *Building your Base* - Talking about physical health to develop healthy body image and establish self esteem and confidence with Be You Challenge
2. *Mental and Emotional Health* - Developing decision making skills, practicing how to deal with activities, writing your personal story
3. *Unleash your Superpowers - Relationship building* - Recognizing and releasing your superpowers, character development
4. *Superhero Missions* - Embracing your superhero mission - going after your goals and dreams, personal growth success tips, affirmations and superhero pledge to building your inner superhero

By the end of this workbook you will create your very own inner superhero. You can take this picture with you anywhere. You can put it up in your locker, on your mirror, in your journal, keep it in this book - wherever you would like. When you face a challenge or want to achieve a goal in life, I want you to remember the power of your inner superhero. I want you to remember that you are not alone and that you have the personal power to overcome any life challenge and achieve any life dream. You will use pieces of each building block section in creating your inner superhero at the end. Follow my lead.

YOU WILL BE THE COOL KID ON THE BLOCK BY CREATING YOUR OWN SUPERHERO!

Are you ready to build and uncover your inner superhero?

Let's do this.

"I've been self-taught since 1989."

Before we dive in, I want you to know and understand some key principles to learning development of personal growth and personal power. First, we must believe in ourselves and know that we have the intelligence to teach ourselves any skill and behaviour. We must know that we have the power to learn, apply, and practice new information at any time in our life. Learning is a lifelong process, and so it's important to know how we learn and what our best learning style is. I want you to know that if something is possible on this planet, then that means it's possible for you.

"We are naturally designed for growth."

Now, the same truth applies when looking at unlearning behaviours. Sometimes we must let go of the old to bring in the new. As human beings we only have so much time, personal energy, and mental clarity. Our capacity and space to hold specific information is vast; however, we must know and be aware that when we release an old behaviour, pattern, or habit that is no longer serving us, it opens us up to experience something new that can fulfill our needs, wants, and desires. You have the intelligence, strength, and power to create the lifestyle you want to live. You have the power to create and un-create by cultivating your own personal power which everyone has.

As human beings we are naturally born and designed to unlearn behaviours and thoughts that are no longer serving our health or happiness. I know this truth because of personal power, my own experiences, and watching the success of others taking courses on psychology and sociology.

"Celebrate your own personal power development."

The reality is we have been self-taught since we were born.

When a teacher or student or peer teaches you something, then we choose whether or not to learn the skills or behaviour.

When I coach, train, and speak I make it a habit to enforce the truth of personal power development - you are the person applying the teachings, so remember to give yourself credit and personal power. Without accepting, receiving, and applying the information there would be no change, result, or success. This practice is part of building life skills such as self esteem, confidence, and strong sense of self. When you learn a new skill or behaviour, by acknowledging and recognizing this truth you will increase your self esteem and confidence. This will inspire you to continue taking steps forward to success. In other words, you are celebrating your own personal power development. BAM!

Life Skills to Last a Lifetime

The teachings you are about to engage in are fabulous to develop inner strength, self esteem, self worth, self respect, self love, self trust, self belief, confidence, and personal power. Truthfully, the possibilities of personal development are endless. The focus with these teachings is to empower you to know that you can achieve any life goal or dream and overcome any life challenge with taking the appropriate action. Whether you are looking at losing weight, making new friends, asking a boy or girl out on a date, earning that scholarship, making the sports team, landing a job, building your mental and emotional health to overcome depression or anxiety, enhancing body image and love for self, or attending a college or university, you have the personal power within to achieve these goals. We are going to build that power throughout this workbook.

What we desire to grow, awaken, or build already exists within us.

The truth of the matter is that the life skills we desire to build and enhance already exist within us. For example, when we discuss self esteem and confidence, it is critical to know and understand that we already have these desired qualities within us. I've heard girls say that their friend doesn't have self esteem or confidence because of the choices they have been making in life. However, the truth is their friend does have self esteem and confidence - but their friend's emotion is at a low level. What needs to happen is to focus on the truth: while there is self esteem and confidence, there is not enough to make healthy decisions. Therefore, our goal and mission is to increase, build, or power up the self esteem and confidence so that we can begin to make decisions and choices out of a place of power. This brings us health and happiness.

When we focus on the positive, more positive will surface.

So if this person is you or if you know someone going through this, focus on the positive qualities within you or them by engaging in positive self talk (I have affirmations for you throughout the workbook) and life activities that you enjoy and that feel good to do. Hang around people who have healthy self esteem and confidence, and you will pick up their energy. Know that the desired life skills you want are within you. Your goal and focus is to magnify and draw them out with your environment, activities, and people in your life. Before you know it, you will feel the mass amounts of pure self esteem and confidence or whatever your desired life skill is. The goal is to build up your inner superhero. I dare you to do it! Keep reading; you will see more about what I mean throughout the building blocks!

Leading by Example

I am a BIG believer in leading by example; therefore, I will share some personal and professional stories on these topics to inspire you to do your activities. This is my commitment to you to inspire you to do the life work. Does this sound fair? Let's Do This!

WE ARE GOING TO BUILD, GROW, AND MAGNIFY YOUR PERSONAL POWER BY BUILDING YOUR INNER SUPERHERO THROUGH THE NEXT FOUR BUILDING BLOCKS! ARE YOU READY TO TAKE SOME ACTION TO MAKE SOME CHANGES IN YOUR LIFE THAT WILL EMPOWER YOU TO KNOW YOU CAN LIVE THE LIFE OF YOUR DREAMS?

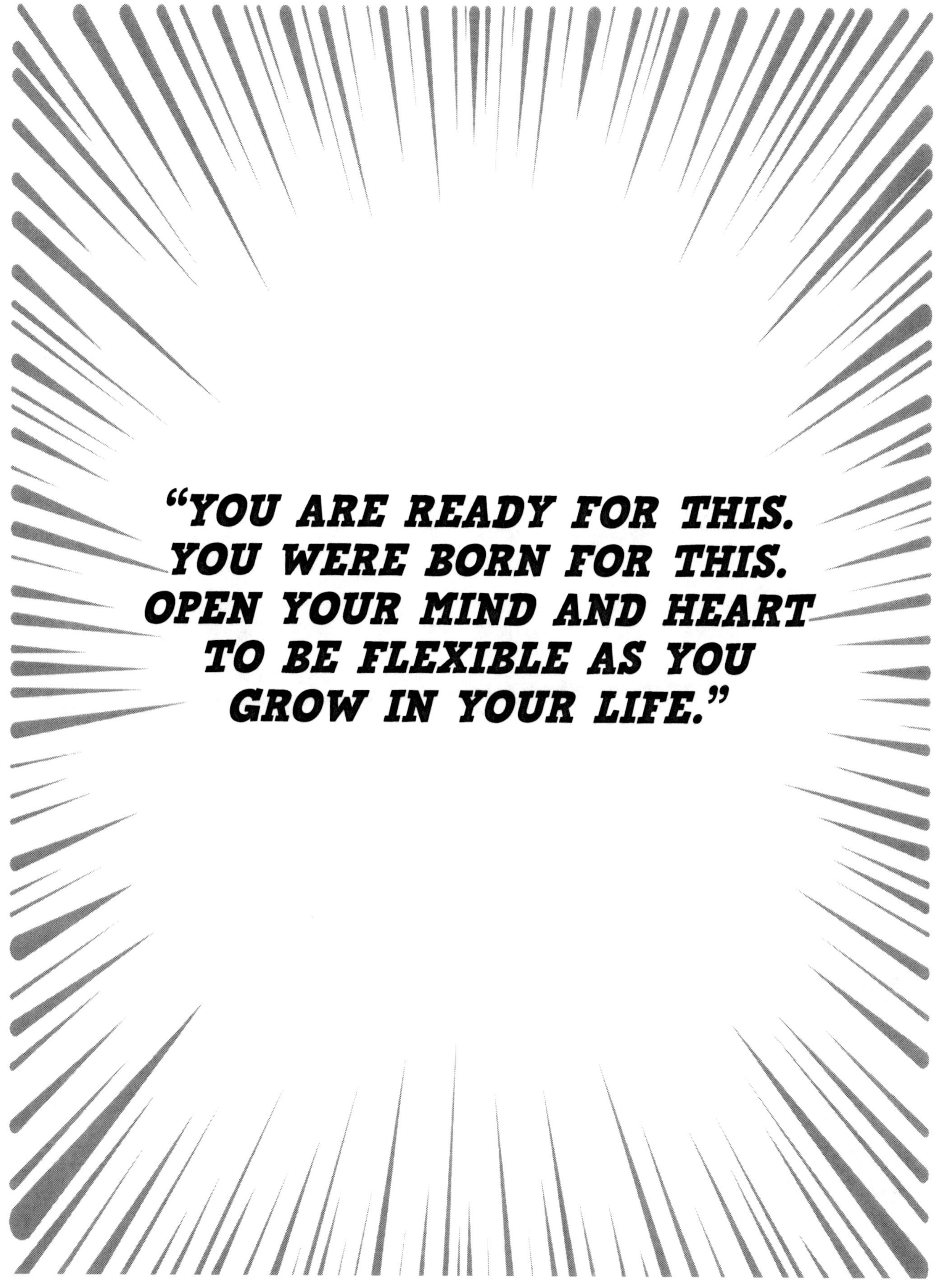
"YOU ARE READY FOR THIS.
YOU WERE BORN FOR THIS.
OPEN YOUR MIND AND HEART
TO BE FLEXIBLE AS YOU
GROW IN YOUR LIFE."

PERSONAL
GROWTH IS WHY
WE ARE HERE!

Inner Superhero Personal Growth Success Tips!

The formula I am introducing to you will guide you toward the best experience for personal growth results.

Formula:

Knowledge + Application = New Discovery (new information)

I want you to use and remember the techniques you've learned from the previous chapters and remember the above formula. You will find these techniques useful in your superhero growth challenges.

Let's celebrate our uniqueness and individuality.

It is important to remember that every human being has their own experience. Like we discussed in the Superhero decision- making formula and how to deal with life events section, two people can observe the same life event, yet walk away with two different memories. No one is right or wrong; it is a matter of perception. As I love sharing experiences with others, remember to celebrate your own personal power and individual experience.

You may find that you enjoy some of these challenges and some you may not. That is okay. My intention with sharing these inner superhero growth challenges is to wake up your inner superhero. Take action to create your own challenges that are specific to your individual growth, needs, goals, and dreams.

"Creating your own specific growth challenges signifies that your inner superhero is awake and in the driver's seat."

For example, you may participate in a challenge that inspires you further by giving you an idea of another challenge you want to implement into your life - a challenge that is key for your growth.

DO IT. Write it down in your journal, calendar, or wherever you will remember to put it into action! Remember, Follow Up is critical to success. Fortune is in the Follow Up :)

Feel free to share and engage in these activities with others. However, if you can't find someone to do them with, don't let that stop you. I did most of these challenges by myself. These challenges will allow you to develop your inner superhero and superpowers by being the leader of your life.

Erica's Tips to Ensure a Fabulous Growth Experience

I want to set you up with successful expectations. I want to be crystal clear on what you can expect so that you can be prepared. Have you noticed that when you prepare for tasks they seem to be a little easier? Same concept applies here. Read the following to set yourself up for success. I believe in you!

I like to characterize the experience like this... challenges are like what they sound: they are challenges. They are areas of growth. This means that there are going to be moments outside of your comfort zone where you may feel unsure, scared, or maybe even anxious. That is okay. You are feeling these emotions for a reason: you have the opportunity to grow. Nothing in life is perfect. So feel these emotions and move forward anyways. Feel the emotions and BE THE SUPERHERO you want to be. DO THE ACTIVITIES. I promise the reward is SO worth it at the end. I promise you were born to face your fears and move through the uncomfortable emotions to achieve your dreams and goals.

Note: It is possible to feel scared, excited, sad, and happy all at once. I want you to feel the emotion you are having a hard time with and embrace it! I want you (Your Inner Superhero) to BE there for your fears and anxiety and give yourself the attention, support, guidance, love, friendship, etc. that you need to follow through on the challenge.

Note: Eliminate being hard on yourself. I remember going through some of these challenges and working through my feelings of insecurity, loneliness, fear, embarrassment, etc.

Be cautious of unsupportive people. It is true that when people are doing the life work of leading a healthy life that others may feel insecure. Let them. I challenge you to lead by example as that is the best communication to give someone who is unsupportive. Be careful about how much energy you give these people as they are in pain themselves. They don't know how to be happy for themselves, so how could they possibly be happy for you? Don't worry; you are not alone. Everyone goes through it.

We are moving onward and upward! Let's do this!

Erica's Growth Visualization Story

I visualize inner growth like biking or running up a steep hill.

I used to look at the hill as being too tall and too far, and I would give up. Then I would remember my goals to rise up. I knew I had to push through. Deep down I knew I had the power.

Once you get going you will arrive at a settling point where you realize this isn't so bad. Everyone has this settling point, whether they realize it or not. Then you will start to experience results, results which keep motivating you. You can take breaks and create checkpoints along the way to power up, reflect, celebrate, and release any negativity not serving you. Once you get up there you feel soooo good for making it! You have just built inner resilience, self esteem, and confidence. You have just grown and you will never lose what you just learned. You will take your skills and experience to the next level of growth, whatever that may be for you. Once you are at the top of the hill, you then get to run down the hill, feeling sooo amazing about your accomplishment. You have just increased your threshold, so the next time you go up the hill it will be a little easier because you are stronger.

YOUR LIFE CHALLENGES AWAIT YOU.

WILL YOU ACCEPT THE CALLS TO ACTION?

I've organized these challenges all throughout this workbook and into the following categories for you: Relationship Building, Community, Self Discovery, and my Personal Awakening Superhero timeline.

LET'S LEVEL UP WITH OUR GROWTH.

What levels of growth are available for us?

Growth happens on multiple levels of living. Think about it: we have our minds, bodies, and souls. In other words, we have our physical, mental, emotional, and spiritual growth that need attention and care. How do we grow in these areas? How do we take care of our needs? I will cover explanations and activity examples in the following chapters.

"Life is simple. Face fear. Go outside your comfort zone. Engage in new experiences. Enhance your happiness. Growth will take you to new places, people, and opportunities."

"Be a player in the game called life. It's yours to be played. Create fun."

I dare you to go live your life to the fullest! Push through the fear and move forward with the feeling of fear there or not. Go engage in a NEW activity today! Growth awaits you :)

PHYSICAL HEALTH BUILDING YOUR BASE AND FOUNDATION FOR LIFE!

Building your Base

I call building a healthy body image building your base. Your base is your body which is your physical shell protecting your body organs and bodily processes. Your body is the home of your soul. Our bodies naturally age with time as they are the vehicles for our experiences. We must nurture and take care of our bodies because if we do not, we will at some point in life experience health issues or diseases - and let's be honest, it is way more fun to feel confident, healthy, and happy :)

"All superheroes feel strong, healthy, and happy with their base, most of the time!"

Note: Let's be real. Life isn't perfect. It was the mentality of thinking it was that held me back from pursing personal growth. What this means is that you feel healthy and happy most of the time!

In this section, I am going to cover how to establish a healthy body image, discuss body image influences, and provide self esteem and confidence activities that will build and enhance your body image. I will talk about the four components of a health workout for your fitness regime, discuss fitness activities, and share some my favourite healthy super foods and drinks that nurture your body and give you the energy to do the activities and participate in life. Get ready to unleash your inner superhero within you.

As you enhance your knowledge on this subject you will see that developing and building a healthy body image is more than just a goal: it is a life skill.

My purpose with this section is for you to build and enhance the following life skills:

- Enhance your confidence to feel comfortable in your own skin through being able to look yourself in the mirror with love and confidence.
- Power up your body image IQ to understand how society and media influence you in identifying your personal body image.
- Identify your individual body type and respect and celebrate your natural body type.
- Dream up fitness goals and see my FAV. super foods that give energy and support the development of your physical body.
- Be You Challenge - Self Care Activity Challenge + Facebook Group for Accountability! Challenge!
- Form game plan action steps to strengthen your body image.

GET READY TO POWER UP!

My body image story

Allow me to be real. There was a time when I didn't like my body. I thought I was ugly and didn't think that any boy would like me the way I was, but most importantly I didn't like me the way my body was. When a boy I liked was interested in me and wanted to hang out, I remember acting weird. I was thinking why would he like me? I self-sabotaged by not thinking I was good enough, when deep down I truly wanted to get to know him. He eventually thought I wasn't interested and moved on. (inner villain and inner superhero in conflict here.)

In school, I got teased for my eyes being too small and wearing glasses. I felt so unhappy that I put my glasses on the driveway so that my dad would run over them when he came home. I didn't want to wear my glasses anymore. I felt sad because I thought my eyes were ugly. I allowed other people's opinions to affect my self esteem and confidence. Interestingly enough, today I LOVE wearing glasses (I find they are studious) and I LOVE my eyes because they are unique.

As I mentioned earlier, there was a period in my life when I committed self harm and abused my body with drugs and alcohol because I had low body image and low self esteem and didn't know how to deal with the past events. I lacked self-love and self-respect. I didn't like the person I was, and so I was self-hating. At this point in my life, my inner villain outweighed my inner superhero.

How did I develop a healthy self esteem, self worth, and body image? I am going to share with you what helped me and my clients develop and grow a healthy body image as we grew through body image pains and challenges. I want you to develop the highest self-love, self-esteem, and self-respect for you and your body! I truly believe that every single one of us human beings is born perfect! Our imperfections make us perfect because nothing is perfect, if you know what I mean :)

As a speaker, life coach, and fitness professional, I've worked with countless women who have struggled with body image at least one point in their lives. I would like to share a few stories with you of women I coached who achieved a high level of body image and healthy living. For the sake of confidentiality, I am going to change the names of these ladies.

Read Martha's Story

"I was always a thin girl, felt fairly comfortable in my skin, and have gone to the gym in fits and spurts since I was a teenager. I have however, struggled with being able to truly understand what my body looks like. Even though I was thin, I would look in the mirror and think I was overweight. That fear of being 'big' kept me from living a fairly healthy life. In my early twenties, after the death of my mother, something in my life and health changed drastically. I lost interest in myself, my health, and frankly most things I used to enjoy in life. From then on I battled a monster... depression. After the first class with Erica, she pushed me and encouraged me to push through the pain. I was worried and scared that I would always be in this pain. After the second class, I felt this power come from within myself to push through, a power that I never thought was possible to come out. Erica told me about the Be You Challenge. I thought a team of supportive women striving towards similar goals was fantastic to keep me accountable. I formed relationships with others going through similar life struggles. My mood and energy levels have increased exponentially. I now look in the mirror and love what I see. I am proud of myself, and so is my family and friends. I am so motivated to continue this new healthy lifestyle that I have signed up for another eight weeks of sessions with Erica. I am so thankful to have met Erica and look forward to working her again."

As you read, Martha knew that to change her life she had to step up and take action. She woke up her inner superhero through taking action. Her action was fitness.

I love stories because I find we can truly learn through other people's stories. We can relate and learn. But for me, most importantly we realize that we are not alone.

Truth: If it is possible on this planet it is possible for you! I challenge you to cultivate this attitude: If Erica and Martha can do it, you can do it!

Read Stephanie's Story

"I am so thankful to have a coach like Erica who really cares about the results and works hard to see the results her clients want to see. Erica has been there every step of the way offering advice and answering questions. I've learned that you get what you put in. Some of us have to put in a little more than others to get the results we want. I've also been very fortunate to be able to share this lesson with other ladies at class and hope that it inspired them to work hard and look beyond the reflection in the mirror or the number on the scale. I look forward to pushing myself at every session. At the end of eight weeks of working together, I lost 10 lbs, 4% of body fat, 18.75 inches, and increased my self-esteem, confidence, energy, and relationships with family and friends."

Aren't these ladies' stories wonderful? I love these stories. Now I ask you: what are you going to take away from their stories?

Your take-aways:

____

____

____

____

Erica's take-aways:

What I LOVE about Martha's story is the power of taking action by being open and honest about her situation and how talking about her situation brought her to success. What I LOVE about Stephanie's situation is how she knew that everyone has their own timeline and journey to achieving goals and how she looked beyond the numbers on the scale. Stephanie looked forward to progress with everyone session and felt the benefits of feeling full of self esteem and confidence!

Now it is your turn to do some life work and reflection.

What is Body Image?

When I typed in body image into Google, the following definition came up: body image is the picture or mental image of one's body.

Where does the perception of body image come from? For most this comes from society definition.

What is Society's Idea of Healthy Body Image?

As you know, I am not a fan of playing the blame game because it takes away my personal power. However, it is important to talk about the reality of body image. We learn body image at a very young age. For me, a lot of the impressions I formed came through movies, music, magazines, shopping malls, etc.

There is no doubt that there are a lot of pressures to look a certain way through society's eyes. Let's talk about society's role in healthy body image. If you go to Google and type in beauty, you are going to see pictures of one kind of person. Thin, makeup, flawless skin, skinny, etc. *Come on, Google, can we get REAL already?! :)* If you watch movies you almost always see perfect looking actors and actresses. If you pick up a magazine you will see something similar.

Happiness, self esteem, confidence, and development of healthy body image starts on the inside: it starts within. Straight up! This is the real deal, I promise!

I can't stress this enough how unreal and unrealistic these photos are. These photos are manufactured through various technologies that enhance the physical features and qualities. It is important to be knowledgeable and to understand the truth that no one naturally looks perfect! The perceptions of the media can be damaging to people's self esteem, confidence, and idea of body image because people allow these unrealistic identities to be something they strive for. It can become an never ending battle, because these goals are not realistic.

Story Time!

I had a client who invested massive amounts of money into getting plastic surgery. But no matter the plastic surgery she underwent, she was not happy. It was a behaviour similar to a drug addiction. She needed to keep replacing the treatments to feel worthy. What she didn't realize was that happiness starts from within. She kept trying to fix how she felt on the outside for something she felt was missing on the inside. She still struggles with these challenges today.

I challenge you to focus on developing your self esteem and confidence, not just physically on the outside with fitness, but focus on what makes you happy in the inside too!

"Let's get real, world. There are three main natural body types, not just the skinny girl version."

As a fitness professional, I studied these body types and taught these concepts to educate others on the truth of body image so that people can learn to embrace and accept their bodies as they are, in their most natural form - to celebrate our uniqueness and originality :)

Allow me to break down the following body types and explain how each type responds to the effects of exercise.

Ectomorph: Difficulty gaining weight, fast and efficient metabolism.

Mesomorph: Losing fat is easy, efficient metabolism, gaining muscle is easy, responds quickly to exercise.

Endomorph: Slow metabolic rate, attacks of tiredness and fatigue, loses weight slowly.

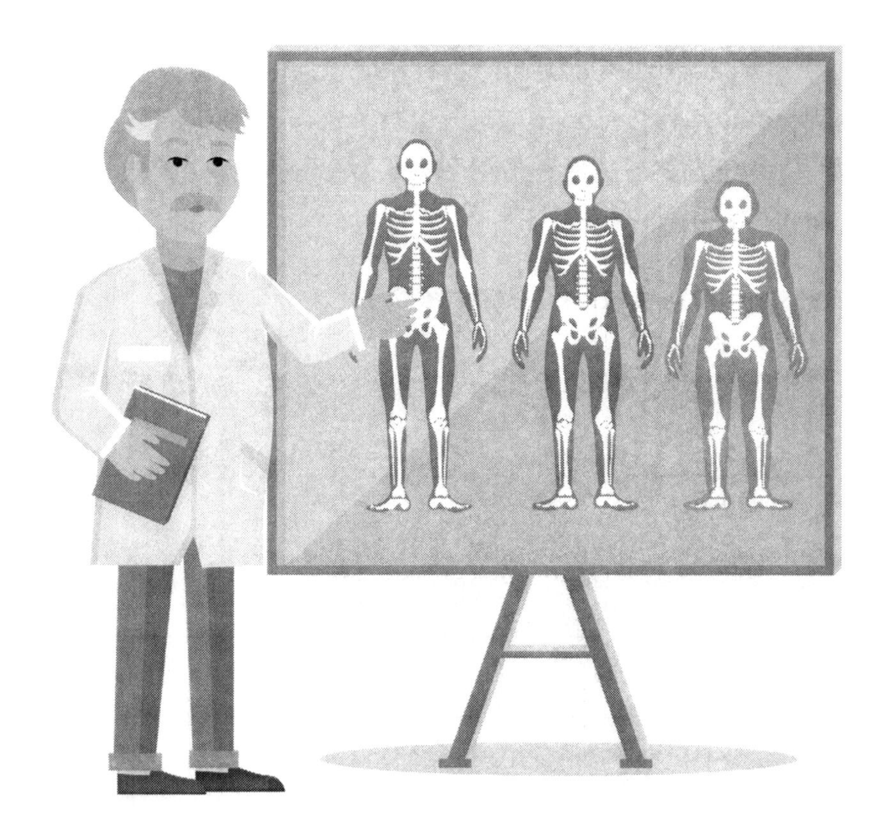

Which body type are you? How happy are you with your natural body type? It's okay to want to see some healthy changes to your body image. Maybe you want to build some muscle, increase your strength, lose some weight, feel more energized, or build self-esteem and confidence so that you can feel better about your body the way it is. What is important is to be real with yourself and understand that everyone is born with a specific body type. I challenge you to find your gifts and embrace your natural body type. Find love for who you are today! Finding love for your body can be one of your superpowers!

Now that we have established what society's perception of body image is and the REAL reality of body types, let's shift our focus to what YOUR current reality and perception of your body image is. Let's dig deep and get real :)

NOTE: Developing a healthy body image is a valuable life skill that needs cultivation. It is rare for someone to already feel good about themselves. We often have to learn how to love our bodies. It's okay to feel insecure about your body. Almost every human being goes through this. So I want you to know that you are not alone in this. I want you to know that in order to experience true, long lasting, love for your body features, you must take consistent action to feel good about who you are in your body :)

Let's focus on some areas of growth:

Write down three qualities you love about your body and why.

____

____

____

____

Erica's Examples:

Three qualities that I love about my body are my eyes because they are unique and I love my smile. I smile often, so I get to feel the happiness shining through. I love my hair; it is long and shiny. I like how I can change hairstyles to reflect my clothes. I can change how I look based on how I feel simply by changing my hairstyle. I like my nails. I love that I can dress them up and colour them to match my outfits.

Write down any qualities or features you do not like about your body and explain why.

____

____

____

____

Erica's Examples:

Today, because of the life work and healthy body image development I've done, I am happy to report that I LOVE every inch of my BODY! and it FEELS so POWERFUL! So I am going to share with you some examples about my body that I didn't like in the past. Next, I will share with you HOW I shifted from not liking to loving my body parts!

In the past,

1. I didn't like my eyes because kids made fun of me.
2. I didn't like my breasts because kids made fun of mine being small.
3. I didn't think my face was perfect enough. I thought I had too many blemishes and skin care issues. In magazines, movies, and music videos everyone looked like they had perfect skin.

Now, we are going to reverse the thought pattern!

I want you to take time to focus on WHY you LOVE those body parts of yourself.

____

____

____

____

Erica's Examples:

How I found love for these body parts I didn't like:

1. I realized how unique my eyes were. Not many people have eyes like mine; they are original! Today, I get so many compliments on my eyes.
2. I learned to accept the size of my breasts for what they were and love them.

3. I learned that we are not perfect - I accepted what is... the following topic allowed me to truly see the reality of healthy body image which aided in my acceptance and allowed me to love my body.

"A key to success is to think your way into results."

Focusing on putting out the intention of loving your body parts that need development is crucial for change. You will feel like you are experiencing two emotions. Feel the hurt and focus on sending love anyways! Trust me... it works :)

* We are practicing using your inner superhero to send LOVE to your inner villain through this process. This is where the power comes from - taking action to transform your inner pain or resistance. *

Time to Take Action to achieve your body image goals!

The Power of Fitness

It is so empowering to build a healthy body through fitness that results in a healthy body image. I have empowered many clients through teaching fitness and life coaching. As many continued to work with me month after month and year after year, I watched them transform themselves through building healthy bodies and minds. I heard stories about the relationship building in their lives that brought them so much happiness. It is no secret that when we feel good about ourselves and our bodies, we have stronger relationships with others. When we feel happiness and are full of love and energy, then we are nicer to others. We have more joy within ourselves, which means we have more joy to share with others. I have witnessed many success stories. To break it down, I have seen the development of healthy body esteem along with love for self and confidence. I've even witnessed marriages that have been saved, addictions that have been healed, depression and anxiety energies that have transformed into love and healthy self esteem, friendships that have formed, and fundraising efforts for charities based on working toward living a healthy and happy lifestyle.

How long does it take to achieve a healthy body image goal?

For some body types, achieving particular goals are easier than others. For some it takes longer to achieve the goal. The timeframe depends on the type of goal and the consistent action that is taken towards achieving the desired goal. Regardless, the power comes from knowledge and creating a game plan to achieve your goal. I got your back! This is my expertise. Are you ready? Let's do this!

Let's establish your body image goals!

What is your own definition of healthy body image?

____

____

____

____

My definition of a healthy body is loving my body no matter the shape, size, or condition it is in. I love my body unconditionally and understand that imperfections are a natural part of life. I embrace and accept my body at all times. I love my body!

What are your body image goals? Include fitness and lifestyle goals.

____

____

____

____

Examples of body image and fitness goals:

- Lose weight, increase energy levels, eat healthier, quit smoking, feel less anxiety, grow through depression, tone and shape your body through building muscle, etc.

Erica's Goals: My body image goals are to love my body no matter what. I will treat my body with respect and love. I learned how to love my eyes, my skin, and the size of all my body parts despite other people's opinions. Since developing this strong body image, my focus has transformed to helping others establish their own strong body images. In addition, I have chosen more fitness goals rather than focusing on the physical body image goals. I would like to complete a triathon and run a half-marathon next because I choose to focus on the feeling of fitness rather than the physical appearance.

How will you measure success? How will you know when you are successful with your body image goals?

____

____

____

____

Erica's Success Measure:

I measure success by progress. I measure success by how I feel about myself. I consider how I feel in my own skin and clothing, but most importantly I think about how I build relationships. I use the mirror technique that I am about to share with you. I measure how comfortable I feel about looking at my body in the mirror and the level of self-esteem and self-worth I have - self talk. I will cover this in more detail in the self-esteem section.

The Power of Physical Fitness to Build a Healthy Body Image

Engaging in fitness activities is a great way to build a healthy body image while enhancing self-esteem and confidence! There are so many different types of physical fitness activities. I challenge you to find some that you like. In this section I am going to have you think about fitness activities you can do that will help with building confidence, self-esteem, and a healthy body image. Next I will explain to you the four core components of a healthy, strong, successful workout: warm up, strength training, cardio training, and flexibility training. Feel free to contact me if you have any questions by going to my website. www.ericahumphrey.com.

Before I dive into the goods, I would like to share some more success stories with you.

Here is Susan's Story:

"Thank you Erica Humphrey. I couldn't have done it without you.

First, you helped me assess my fitness level and set specific fitness goals. You also identified areas that I didn't know I needed help with (cardio and core strength, for instance).

Second, you designed exercise routines that helped me succeed. You taught me the proper order, technique, and timing for specific exercises. You also modified my routines to keep it interesting and avoid plateaus. They were challenging, but not impossible. I was amazed at my process.

Third, I really appreciate the way you kept me focused and encouraged fitness to become a part of my lifestyle. The nutrition journaling, emails, helpful articles, Saturday boot camp, and the charity stair climb up the tallest building in London all helped make fitness a natural part of the everyday.

Fourth, you were always positive and never doubted my ability to succeed. You were always willing to answer questions, and I felt you were 'there for me' - even outside of the gym appointments.

I attained a fitness level beyond my expectation (I can run for thirty minutes!).

As I work in the U.S. over the next three months, I will be able to stay on top of my goals with the training you gave me."

Read Charlene's Story:

"Erica is the reason I keep showing up. She helps keep my spirits up. Erica is so full of life and eager to explore possibilities that each person has. She is always searching for new things that I can challenge myself with. I've lost weight and improved my heart health, happiness, and strength. Thank you Erica!"

What Fitness Activities Do You Love or Want to Try?!

What Fitness Activities do you enjoy doing? What new fitness activities do you want to try?

____

____

____

____

Erica's Examples:

* Running
* Biking
* Walking
* *Yoga - I participate in yoga to release emotions like anxiety and depression. I am in love with yoga and practice often :)*
* I LOVE to try the latest fitness class and style like P90x and Insanity and Orange Theory Fitness
* Strength training
* Hiking through the forest
* Canoeing and Kayaking
* Skating
* Snowboarding
* Golfing

* Organized events like Run for the Cure

Call to Action!

Pick three activities that you love and schedule them on your calendar. You want to schedule three activities over the next month! Get Ready GO! Feel free to share with me on Facebook or send an email sharing what activities you did and how they felt! I would LOVE to hear :)

Four Components of a Healthy Workout!

When Working Out it is important to incorporate the following types of workouts to ensure healthy and successful exercise:

Warm Up - The warm up is intended to warm up the muscles that you are going to work to prevent injuries and build stamina and endurance by preventing fatigue and mentally getting you in the zone for your upcoming workout. How should your warm up feel? Just like it sounds, it should feel warm. This is a not an intense burst of energy. You want to feel about a 6 out of 10 intensity. Warm up for as long as it takes for you to feel the 6 before you go into the next phase of your workout.

Strength Training - Strength training is designed to build muscle and strength to support your posture and give you the energy, power, and strength to more easily live your day-to-day. Building positivity also promotes confidence. Building strength can look physically appealing. As you build muscle, you will look toned and defined and this can give you the feeling of enhanced self-esteem and confidence. Building muscle burns calories so that you can trim off the weight that you desire to lose.

Cardiovascular Heart Training - Cardio is designed to strengthen your heart and endurance. When we strengthen our heart we are building this muscle so that it doesn't have to work as hard to pump blood to the rest of our body. A good test to see where you are at with your heart health is to know your resting heart rate. The lower your resting heart rate the better, because that means your heart is strong and doesn't have to work as hard to pump blood throughout your body.

Flexibility - I LOVE flexibility training. After a workout it feels so good to stretch out the muscles that you just put pressure on. I love to either engage in yoga or else I have a series of stretches I perform after a workout. When we stretch out our muscles we relieve pressure and tension that we put onto our bodies during our workout. Stretching helps with recovery time and releases negative energy like anxiety and depression.

* Before beginning a fitness routine consult a doctor or professional who is well-versed and knowledgeable in these areas. *

TAKE ACTION!
YOU ARE WORTH IT!

What is Self Esteem?

According to Google, self esteem is confidence in one's own worth and abilities and self respect.

"Self esteem is being able to look in the mirror with confidence."

When was the last time you stood looking in the mirror with confidence? I want you to go stand in front of the mirror right now. Yes, that's right, right now. Get up and go stand in front of the mirror and take this book with you :) The goal is to maintain eye contact with you, to send loving vibes to you with your mind, heart, and soul. When I did this the first time I couldn't look at myself in the mirror. I didn't like who I saw in the reflection. I had negative thoughts thinking that I didn't like the size of my body and struggled maintaining eye contact with me. I was beating myself up! After reflecting through meditation and "interviewing" me on why I felt this way, my villain side began to open up. I realized that I was embarrassed and ashamed of the abuse, addictions, and crimes I had committed in the past. No matter the intense emotions of fear and anxiety I felt, I kept doing the mirror work. I knew that I had been thinking negatively about myself for a long time, and that it was going to take some time to reverse the negativity to positivity.

Persistence pays off.

Over time, I began to find this activity fun! I would write little love notes and messages of positivity and love on the mirror with lipstick. Every morning I would look at them and smile.

Engaging in mirror work was critical to my healing to facilitate personal growth with self esteem and confidence.

I used this technique often to check in and see how my self esteem and confidence were building as I went through my transformation activities.

Activity:

When you look in the mirror, what do you see? How do you feel?

____

____

____

____

Body Image + Mirror Activity = Awesomeness

I want you to look back to your body image sheet. Then go look in the mirror and send love to the areas that you feel insecure about. I want you to think and say out loud how much you love you and each one of those body parts. Read what you wrote about why you love them, and see what happens :)

Write down any ideas or thoughts that come up during this exercise.

____

____

____

____

This exercise is powerful!

I would look in the mirror and tell myself how much I love me, how I forgive myself for the past crimes, and how I realize that the abuse wasn't personal to me. The abusers were reflecting to me what they felt inside (as discussed in the beginning session on bullying). I started to feel SO good about myself, I experienced a new confidence, and this behaviour was coming out in real life because I was doing the inner work.

As I mentioned, I participate in this exercise often! I've got to the point of feeling SO comfortable with it, I have conversations with myself. Not as strange as it sounds, I promise. This technique works extremely well in developing your inner superhero because you are learning to be your own coach! I taught this technique and found it very successful in fitness coaching because I would teach clients to be their own coach - This is their personal power! I would show them that they could motivate, teach, and encourage themselves to achieve their fitness and health goals. My purpose is to teach clients how to set themselves up for success long after our sessions were done. I got them ready to self maintain their workouts on their own.

"Like taking a shower, brushing your teeth, and combing your hair, these activities are best practiced daily and as often as possible. As Nike says, JUST DO IT :)"

BE THE PERSON
WHO YOU WANT TO BE

Don't forget your ABCs! Always Be Confident

As you engage in the body image and self esteem reflection question and commit to the exercise and mirror activity, trust that you are building your confidence. BAM!

What is confidence?

According to Google, confidence is a feeling of self-assurance arising from one's appreciation of one's own abilities or qualities.

Confidence to me is loving yourself completely, unconditionally, and undeniably.

-Erica

Confident people get what they want in life.

How do we know when we are confident? How do we recognize when someone else is confident? When we have a strong sense of confidence with our bodies and self esteem, we put out a confidence energy to the world. People who are typically confident with their body image are the ones who are in healthy relationships. Confident people believe in serving others because they know that through empowering others to celebrate their own superpowers they are empowering themselves. Confident people don't allow other people's opinions to hold them back. Confident people ask for help and aren't intimated by other people's success. They celebrate other people's success! They are often the ones who are given opportunities in life - because of their confidence. Confident people know when to say no or no thank you, and they know how to take care of themselves so that they can take care of others.

Naturally, human beings are attracted to confident people - think about it. Look at the leaders in the world; we talked about Gandhi and Mother Teresa. Their confidence in the ability to lead resulted in tremendous life change for thousands of people. There is no doubt that you will see confidence. The great news is that confidence is a life skill that can be learned by anyone, no matter their life experiences, and this confidence can be applied to every aspect of our lives.

How do you know when you are confident?

____

____

____

____

For me, I know I am confident when I feel comfortable in my own skin, when I give people eye contact, when I listen to others, when I am not afraid to share my vulnerabilities and insecurities because we all have them, and when I take action even when I feel afraid because I know the outcome that I want.

#1 Confidence Game Changer!

I built confidence through the power of pushing through my fears!

Erica's Top Three Fears which from pushing through have become the BIGGEST Life CHANGERS!

1. I was scared of public speaking.
   Yes. It is true. I was terrified of public speaking. It wasn't until I was 19 that I gave my first public talk on personal growth. I was so nervous, but I did it anyway. This was the beginning of my desire to pursue public speaking, an activity which I so passionately love today. This is where I get to inspire change in others. I think that facing this fear paid off, what do you think? :)

2. I was scared of attending networking events.
   These networking events formed a platform where I had the opportunity to meet awesome people to network with and where I built my businesses. At one of the events I ended up meeting my business coach who worked with me to achieve the fitness award. The business coach offered me free coaching through a scholarship program. Thanks to facing my fear, I have achieved success on many levels in business and won new fitness clients.

3. I was scared of facing my inner pain from past events.
   I was afraid of facing my inner pain with the truth. I was scared to deal with the pain in a healthy way, and so this pain came out in unhealthy ways. Before facing my inner pain, I was smoking, doing drugs, drinking, arguing often, etc.

However, the truth is that this pain is going to be there no matter what. I can choose to hide or run away from my fear but it will still be there. I chose to be my own fearless superhero to face my abuses and pain. With thought and reflection, I let go of the pain, released it, and then out came my inner superhero. I awoke a force so powerful inside of me that I saved my own life! I saved myself from living in fear for the rest of my life; from struggling; from feeling lost, scared, and confused; and from holding onto emotions of depression and anxiety. I learned how to transform these emotions into positivity.

Ok, now it is your turn :)

What are three of your Biggest Fears and HOW can you push through them anyways?

Remember the acronym of fear: You have a choice on which definition you want to identify with.

Face Everything And Run OR Face Everything And Rise.

Examples on How to Push Through Fear:

- Rely on support resources such as guidance counselor, social worker, parents, teachers, books, websites, courses, etc.

1. ____

How can you push through this fear?

____

____

____

____

2. ____

How can you push through this fear?

____

____

____

____

3. ____

How can you push through this fear?

____

____

____

____

After you have pushed through a fear, celebrate! Reward your behaviour after pushing through a challenging exercise. Schedule in a fun activity that you love to do!

What activities can you engage in to reward yourself for stepping up and pushing through a fear?

____

____

____

____

Confident people know the importance of Self Care!

Engaging in Self Care Activities will strengthen your inner superhero to push through fear and achieve goals. You are powering UP with self care activities!

Self care activities are activities that I just LOVE to engage in! It just feels so good :) Engaging in self-care and enjoyment activities is imperative to unlocking your inner superhero and the key to enhancing your love for yourself, confidence, and self esteem. You will thank yourself for the amounts of self-care you give to you! Trust me :)

There is no better time than the present.

I am about to give you a challenge. Are you ready? It is called Be You Challenge! The challenge is you pick three self care activities to do for you! Yes, that's right, three self esteem activities for you! What three activities are you going to do today?

We are going to drum up some ideas together.
Are you ready? Ok, great!

I have written down 12 of my favourite self esteem and confidence building activities.

1. GO to the GYM! Or take a walk in nature!
2. Cook a delicious meal! I love cooking as I find it therapeutic!
3. Painting is fun for me to release my creativity- I LOVE acrylic painting!
4. Reading puts positive affirmations and stories in my head. It helps to shift my mindset.
5. Visit with a friend over tea or coffee or ask a friend to join me in any of the above activities :)
6. Shed LOVE on the world - random acts of kindness - (buy someone coffee, leave love notes in random places, make cupcakes for a neighbour, create short videos for important people in my life and tell them why I LOVE and appreciate them)
7. Nap IT!
8. Music IT!
9. Massage or dentist! I LOVE the feeling of having my teeth clean!
10. Watch IT! movies, concerts, YouTube videos, etc.
11. Meditate - JUST BE.
12. SMILE - find something to laugh about, make someone else laugh.

KEY TO SUCCESS: There are going to be days when you don't want to do self-esteem activities - these are the days you need to do them the most. The mission here is to create and build strong healthy habits to get you aligned with high levels of self-esteem, confidence, and happiness.

YOUR TURN!!!

Write down your List of 12 Awesome Activities that you want to do to enhance your inner superhero/self esteem and confidence. These can be NEW activities that you haven't done before or existing activities that you've already enjoyed!

READY, SET, TAKE ACTION NOW!

1. ______________________________

2. ______________________________

3 ______________________________

4. ______________________________

5. ______________________________

6. ______________________________

7. ______________________________

8. ______________________________

9. ______________________________

10. ______________________________

11. ______________________________

12. ______________________________

Today, you are going to JUMP START you into Self Care Activities!

Write down the three activities that you are going to do today for your Be You Challenge! Get ready, get set, go!

1. ______________________________

2. ______________________________

3. ______________________________

JOIN THE FACEBOOK GROUP!

Go to Facebook, join the group Be You Challenge, and then message me your three self care activities! I can't wait to hear about it :)

"The best investment you can make is in yourself."

"Be the person you want to see in the world."

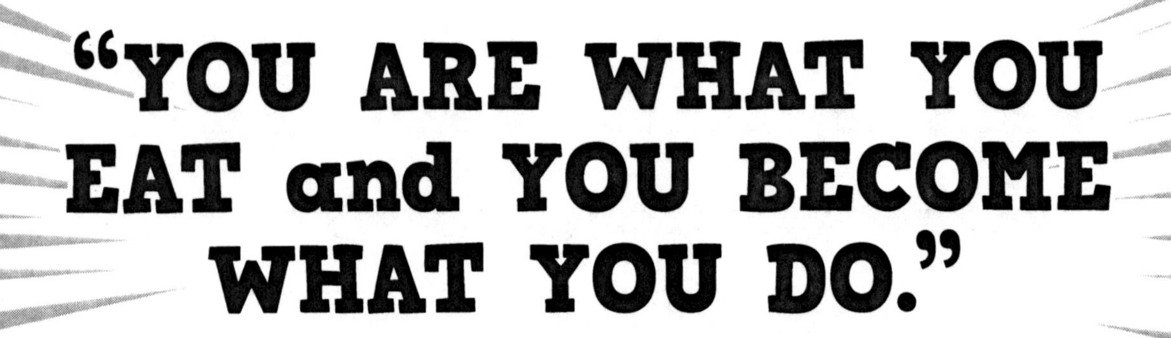
"YOU ARE WHAT YOU
EAT and YOU BECOME
WHAT YOU DO."

Super Foods that Give You Energy

"Fitness + Nutrition are healthy living partners. You need to engage in both to achieve a healthy wellbeing."

Throughout this next portion of the book I am going to share my personal food journal including super foods and drinks I consciously choose to consume to feed my body, the power of food and water, and awesome food affirmations.

I recommend speaking to your parents and teachers about healthy eating. I have attached an example of a food journal that I use to plan out my week. I have attached a blank sheet for you if you want to do the same.

"I challenge you to be your very own NUTRITION SUPERHERO!"

I challenge you to think about how you can use food to ignite your inner superhero. How are you going to have enough energy to achieve life dreams and overcome life challenges if you are not giving your body healthy fuel? How are you going to have enough energy to save your world and be a shining star for others? :)

Let's get real: how are the foods we eat and the way we feel about ourselves connected? How does food have anything to do with our body image, self esteem, and confidence? Simple: It is no secret that the food we eat contains calories and nutrients.

Certain foods contain more calories that affect our body size and weight. Think about your body image goals and the types of foods that are aligned with your body image goals. You want to align yourself with the proper nourishment and energy to sustain your day-to-day activity level and body image goals.

What are Super Foods?

What are super foods and drinks, and how do they give us energy? According to Google, a super food is nutrient-rich food considered to be especially beneficial for health and well-being. I learned the power of foods during my studies of Nutrition and Wellness, Health Coach and Meditation Coach Courses, and through my personal and professional experience. I would coach clients through healthy eating and a fitness regime that worked together to achieve health and fitness goals! However, the power always came from within the client because at the end of the day the client knows what their life schedule is. The client knows what type of meals are realistic to cook, their specific dietary needs, food that feeds their soul, etc.

Taking charge of your eating habits is a life skill.

Nutrition and healthy eating is a life skill that needs to be practiced and developed until you find the right foods for your budget, schedule, mind, body, heart, and soul! I've heard of too many students skipping breakfast and eating unhealthy foods that are high in sugar and other low energy ingredients. These foods do impact how you feel and how your body grows. These foods can affect your attention span, focus, emotions, and body size.

Food Provides positive or negative energies!

The food we eat carries nutrients and positive or negative energies. Think of a time when you ate something and felt tired, lethargic, and sluggish. Then think of a time when you ate something and felt high energy, happy, and positive. It is true; the food we eat affects how we feel.

When we love ourselves, our bodies, our minds, and our hearts, we want to feed ourselves with healthy foods simply because that is what our bodies need and crave. We love to take care of our health!

"When you wake up your inner superhero you wake up to your truth on all levels of living."

Personally, my nutrition AH-HA moment or game changer occurred during the phase of awakening my inner superhero. I learned that my body didn't want to consume foods and drinks that were at a lower energy level. I naturally gravitate towards higher vibration energy foods. These foods helped with the anxiety and depression that I was going through because these foods had a higher energetic vibration that allowed me to raise up my moods. I learned how to use food as a tool to raise my inner energy levels that released the anxiety and depression energy level. Foods truly affect our moods. This experience has been SO POWERFUL for healthy living. I have passed on this information to clients who have seen tremendous results!

Read Danielle's Story

"Meeting Erica and starting to work out with her has been the best thing that I have ever discovered and decided to do. I knew I needed someone else for guidance, support and accountability. One day I came across Erica's information on the internet and something made me send her a message. Erica was encouraging and gave my hope. I was battling with low levels of energy and some depression. Working with Erica's program allowed me to participate in daily activities around self esteem, nutrition, and fitness that changed the way I felt. While trying countless fitness plans, programs, and trainers nothing seemed to work. Erica's real life story and teachings did! I plan to continue practicing Erica's teaching in my day-to-day to keep my energy levels up. Thank you Erica!"

THIS STUFF WORKS!!!

I always LOVE reading these stories! I can tell you it's not to boost my EGO; however, it certainly is nice to see that I did my job! I love reading these stories because these teachings that I have passed on to others WORK! They truly have been life changers for these amazing women and I want YOU to have your own success story too! Everyone has a story and I look forward to hearing yours!

Super Drinks

When I think of super drinks I definitely think of water as the first on my list! I just LOVE Water! Our bodies are made up of over 70% water and water is essential for survival. When clients ask me how much water to drink, I tell them to do the pee test. You want your pee to be clear. How much water depends on your age, environment, fitness and activity level, etc. A good rule of thumb is to drink as much water as possible. For those of you who do not like water as much, I recommend adding some fruit to the mix to change up the taste. I recommend adding lemon, lime, strawberries, other berries, etc.

Another super drink I LOVE is tea! Certain types of tea offer many health benefits for the body. For example, green tea is loaded with antioxidants and nutrients that have powerful effects on the body. This includes improved brain function, fat loss, a lower risk of cancer, and many other incredible benefits.

** I LOVE any drink that tastes good with healthy ingredients and low sugars. The more natural the better!*

Erica's Favourite Foods and Drinks

Feel Good Healthy Foods

- Fruit including all kinds of berries, apples, and bananas
- Vegetables like carrots, cucumber, peppers, hot peppers! (I LOVE anything spicy)
- Boiled eggs - I boil two eggs in the morning. They give me the nutrients I need like protein and the process is fast. I am not a huge morning person, so I appreciate the quick preparation time.
- Avocado - I LOVE making guacamole
- Stir-fry
- Sweet Potatoes
- Chicken and Lamb
- Tofu and red beans
- Seafood pasta
- SALAD! I LOVE all kinds of salad: fruit salad, veggie salad, garden salad, etc.
- hummus and veggies

Feel Good Healthy Drinks

- Tea
- Water - add some lime, lemon, strawberries, cucumber to add some FUN flavour
- Sparkling water
- Beet Juice

- Coconut water
- Lemon water
- Cranberry juice
- Kale Juice
- Pomegranate juice
- Smoothies

Juice: I love pineapple and apple juice - I usually add water to these juices to water down the sugar

Erica's Food Journal

My goal is to eat 80% of the time what I should and eat 20% of the time what I enjoy like snacks, treats and desserts! I drink water constantly throughout the day! I drink water with every meal! Don't like water? Look at my super foods and drink list to naturally flavour your water up!

Breakfast : Eggs + Banana + Black Berries = Happy that I took time to feed me with positive energy to take on the day!

Snack: Granola bar or yogurt or apple

Lunch: I LOVE salads; people will often catch me with a chicken salad or bean salad or dinner leftovers from the night before like chicken stir fry.

Snack: Granola bar or yogurt or apple

Dinner: Whatever I FEEL like making. Sometimes its chicken, seafood, tofu with veggies like carrots and peppers, or Caesar salad made from scratch! Sometimes I cook for others or visit friends or family for dinner.

Snack: Frozen yogurt, ice cream, chocolate, chips, sometimes pop or sparkling water.

How much water did you drink today? My goal is to drink approximately two litres of water per day depending on my activity level and the environment I am in. For example, I drink more water during the summer because I am outside often and active and my body needs to replenish more liquids.

Festive Dinner Parties!

As a part of waking up my inner superhero, I began to fall in love with life experiences. I love participating in creating festive dinner parties with Mexican, Italian, Seafood, or Indian themes! I love doing this to explore different cultures and celebrate the uniqueness and variety in the world!

Positive Affirmations Around Eating

The weekends are when I usually tend to treat myself with pizza, tacos, salsa and chips, desserts, etc. I am consciously aware of the foods that I put into my body. I am aware of what foods are healthy for me that positively impact my mood. I listen to my body and trust my body to guide me to choose foods that are great for my overall well being. I live in moderation and believe in a balanced approach to healthy eating. I am aware that one size does not fit all. I am aware that everyone has their own food truth and knows what is best for them. I choose to live by example with healthy eating for others. Because I LOVE my body so much, I deserve to treat my body with healthy eating and living. I LOVE food!

What are your positive affirmations around eating?

____

____

____

____

Food Journal

Breakfast:

Snack:

Lunch:

Snack:

Dinner:

Snack:

How much water did you drink today?

You can download extra copies from www.ericahumphrey.com

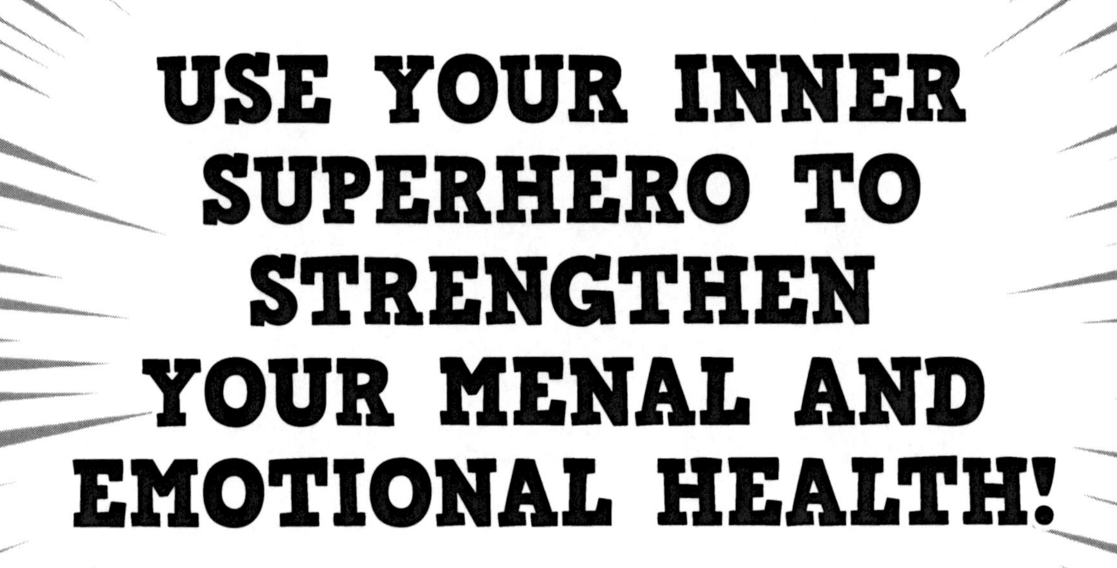
USE YOUR INNER
SUPERHERO TO
STRENGTHEN
YOUR MENAL AND
EMOTIONAL HEALTH!

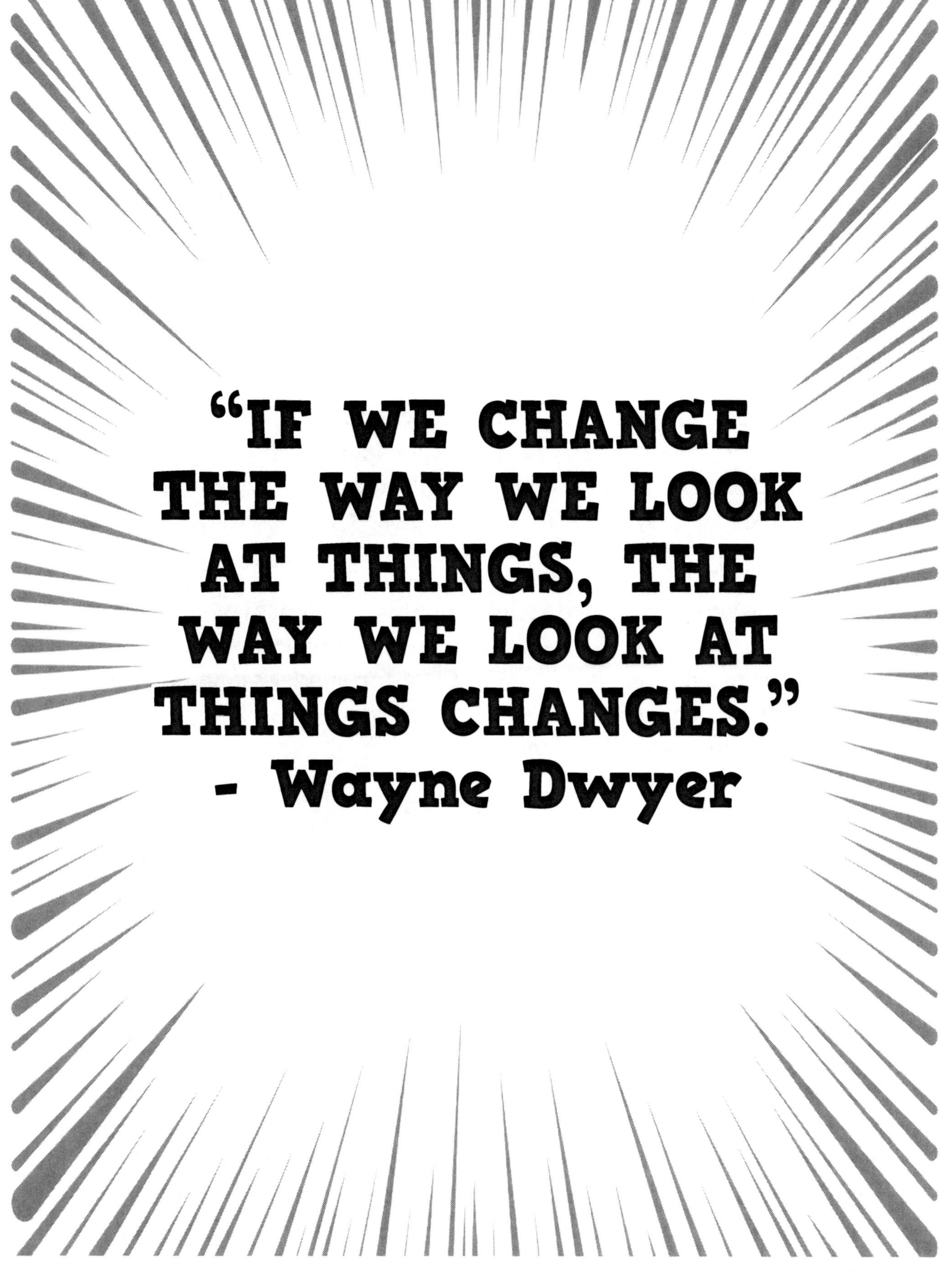
"IF WE CHANGE
THE WAY WE LOOK
AT THINGS, THE
WAY WE LOOK AT
THINGS CHANGES."
- Wayne Dwyer

Mental Health - Mindset Matters

"My Inner Superhero saved me from negative thinking like anxiety, depression, and suicidal thoughts."

"If we change the way we look at things, the way we look at things changes." I love this quote by Wayne Dwyer. He has taught me some great life tools through his books and YouTube videos. His words still inspire me today!

Get ready to read some stories and recognize some amazing life skills that have the power to set you free from negative thinking, bullying, and peer pressure while opening up the door for self esteem, self love, self respect, love, health, and happiness on the mental mindset level.

In this chapter we are going to talk about your mindset, your thought processes, your beliefs, how you make decisions, your internal story or self talk, a decision making formula I use for mindset empowerment, and a "how to deal with life events" exercise that will empower you to feel like your own superhero!

Success Tips

To be crystal clear, the following activities work best when joined with the previous chapter on base. Engaging in physical activity, super foods, and drinks will increase your success rate and shorten your timeframe of achieving your mental health goals. If you do these activities once in a blue moon, you can expect little results. You've got to invest time, effort, and consistency into your health.

I want to share a story with you that involves activating and using my inner superhero. My superhero mission was to create love and self esteem in my life RIGHT NOW! I needed to feel these amazing emotions and fast. There were times of extreme hopelessness and powerlessness. I felt so unhealthy and unhappy and I needed to change those emotions asap! Through prayer (ask and you shall receive) I asked for guidance from a higher power. That's when I naturally stumbled upon the discovery of how to change my emotions with my thoughts, because the technique I am about to share with you gave me results right away.

Let's Do This!

I learned how to build my mental health through the power of mental self awareness, and then I learned how to choose and select which thoughts I wanted to focus on. I first learned this power by noticing how amazing I felt one moment and negative the next moment when there was no significant life event - just a trigger. I questioned what had created the shift and noticed that my thoughts had changed. I sat down and focused on shifting my thoughts to be fun-loving, and when I did this, my feelings changed. I felt like I had just found gold. This was a superpower I could now use anytime I chose to.

"I learned how to give the inner villain's mental power to my inner superhero."

This technique helped me to overcome depression, anxiety, and negative thinking. I realized that I was able to activate a power behind the thoughts that allowed me to choose and recreate new thoughts aligned with my goals, dreams, and desires.

Let's put this theory into practice!

We are going to do a Mental Health Check!

I want you to pay attention to what you are thinking about. How do you feel right now? What are you thinking about? Do you know that thoughts create emotions? My question to you is what are you feeling on a scale of 1 to 10 in terms of happiness?

Write down how you are feeling right now. How happy are you on a scale of 1- 10?

____

____

____

____

What thoughts are you aware of that are creating your emotions right now?

____

____

____

____

We are now going to purposefully and intentionally choose thoughts that are aligned with self esteem, confidence, self love, and health.

Affirmations

Now I want you to read and focus on the affirmations below, and then ask yourself the same questions!

"What I concentrate on is exactly what I will attract. Joy brings joy."

"I am a bright, capable person. With my thoughts, I can create an ever more rewarding life."

"Yesterday is done and gone. Today is the first day of my future."

"I view all experiences as opportunities for me to learn and grow."

"I know that all is well, and even better things are coming to me."

"I give to others all the things I want to receive. In this way, we bless and prosper each other."

"Today I choose to see my life as an adventure. I uproot outdated beliefs and discover hidden treasures of joy and freedom."

"Each day I express more fully the inner beauty and strength of my true being."

"I do something new – or at least different – every day."

"I am part of the Universe; therefore, I know that there is an order, rhythm, and purpose to my life."

"I am grateful for Life's generosity. I am so blessed."

"I get plenty of sleep every night. My body appreciates how I take care of it."

"I was born for a purpose. I deserve to feel loved, accepted, appreciated, and respected. I am worthy of love, health, happiness, and success. I choose the definitions of these words and I choose to live the life I was born to live!"

Write down how you are feeling right now. How happy are you now on a scale of 1-10?

____

____

____

____

What thoughts are you aware of that are creating your emotions right now?

____

____

____

____

Did you notice a shift? The next time you feel a low energy I want you to practice this exercise. I want you to focus on choosing positive thoughts and energy to shift your emotions.

Note: This practice is not about suppression; instead, it is about being real with your emotions and mental health. Don't worry, this exercise takes practice. As I mentioned before, the more you do this the stronger the results will be. Keep Practicing to build this into a habit!

You can choose to align with your inner superhero or your inner villain. Focus on the positive thoughts and they will lead to positive outcomes. Thoughts are just that - thoughts. You have the power to choose to align with them or make decisions from your thoughts and feelings.

The path to least resistance moves forward.

The path to least resistance is the best path to take. Start with something that gives you a result right away. Focus on the result because what you focus on grows. This will build your self esteem, confidence and personal power.

If this feels uncomfortable or unnatural for you, that is okay! Keep practicing until you reach success - until you reach a result you are happy with.

Incorporating affirmations into my daily routine has been and still is a life changer for me and others. I challenge you to write out and read affirmations that are aligned with your personal goals and dreams.

Write out affirmations for your life goals and dreams!

____

____

____

____

"Mental and Emotional Health are partners - One can't be healthy without the other."

What is mental and emotional health?

When I Googled the definition of mental health, I found this: noun: mental health a person's condition with regard to their psychological and emotional well-being.

A useful definition of emotional wellbeing is offered by the Mental Health Foundation: "A positive sense of wellbeing which enables an individual to be able to function in society and meet the demands of everyday life; people in good mental health have the ability to recover effectively from illness, change."

Emotional Intelligence is a Life Skill!

Have you noticed that feelings come and go? This is why it is important to make decisions out of a place of your superhero... this is beyond the emotional reactions... this is a place where your decisions are aligned with who you truly are.

For years I was used to making decisions out of my inner villain's emotions. My emotions truly controlled me. I was not emotionally aware and my emotional intelligence was low. When I learned the power of selecting thoughts (the previous exercise), I learned that my emotions were only temporary and that I could shift my thoughts to change how I felt. This ultimately guided me toward making different decisions that led to different outcomes.

When I was younger, I was used to making decision out of emotions of anger, resentment, hurt, sadness, loneliness, fear, etc. As a result of certain choices, I got myself in juvi for physically fighting with others and saying hurtful things that I later regretted. This happened because I was not aware and didn't know how to deal with my emotions. I didn't know how to release them in a healthy way, I didn't know that emotions were temporary, and I didn't know how to shift my thoughts to align with more comfortable emotions.

Let's Be Strong Superheroes Who know HOW to be in control of our emotions. Let's be resilient and Bounce Back from Life!

I want to let you know that by awakening my inner superhero I realized how unhealthy my mental and emotional health was. Before the awakening I was in denial and not open to a conversation about my mental health. My depression, anxiety, suicidal thoughts, and feelings of powerlessness were results of thoughts and these thoughts consumed me often. I would identify with past thoughts. As a result, I would feel like I was paralyzed and not wanting to do anything. I went through cycles of depression. If someone would have noticed these cycles before my awakening, I wouldn't have admitted to it or agreed with that person. I was scared to face my pain - the truth, the embarrassment, and the uncertainty of how the hell I got here. The truth is I wasn't fully ready to face my pain.

"There was an inner battle between my inner superhero and inner villain."

There was a piece of me that wanted to break through the pain and deal with what was going on within me. This was my inner superhero and this side of me was working so hard to break free to save my life!

"I knew I had life work to do, but I didn't know exactly how to do it or what it was."

One thing I KNEW for sure was I wasn't going to accept my life for what it was.

I knew that life couldn't be just this. Life couldn't be all this pain without something greater. Something inside me knew that there was more than this pain. I didn't know what it was, but I was determined and destined to find the answers. So I kept looking and learning until I found what I was looking for.

HOW I STRENGTHENED MY INNER SUPERHERO AND SHONE THROUGH!

Through my personal work of meditation, studying psychology in school, creating my own decision making formula, reflection, and personal silent retreats I was able to cultivate the power of my thoughts organically. I didn't have to take medication to treat my negative thought patterns. I was able to activate my inner superhero by selecting and choosing thoughts which aligned with my health and happiness goals. Throughout my journey to discovering how to build healthy mental thought patterns, there were multiple experiences in my life that "planted seeds". These seeds led to the awareness and awakening and healing of my thoughts. I would put myself into environments that brought me happiness where I could mentally clear my head. This was and still is a process I practice. I engaged in personal growth activities that enhanced my mental and emotional health.

The following activities helped to enhance my mental health:

* meditation

* recognizing that words have power

* therapy and counseling

* reading books

* spending time outdoors

* running/fitness workouts

* openness with a burning desire to find the truth

* being open and willing to try new things and new experiences

* stepping outside my comfort zone through attending conferences, courses, fitness classes, visiting local community centres, networking events, etc.

I experienced many AH-HA moments through engaging in the above activities. Some experiences can only be experienced. I challenge you to go Power Up through taking action towards your mental health.

Fitness was my #1 GO TO!

Oh, how I LOVE fitness. There are countless benefits to physical activity. For example, working out releases healthy endorphins in the brain that give energy and happiness. Working out also gives you time to focus on meditation and awareness of your thoughts. Working out allows you to channel and release any negativity and anger while building positive emotions. I can't tell you how many times I went for a run just to run out my sadness, anger, and pain. Running is just an example of a fitness activity I did to release and channel my feelings in a healthy way as opposed to drinking and doing drugs. I also became aware of negative thoughts that were affecting my mood. I was able to shift them around by choosing to think differently. Fitness was a game changer in the development and health of my mental health.

Words have Power.

Next, I learned the power of words. How and what we say about ourselves has power and influence over how we feel about ourselves and others. Do you remember that saying in school: "sticks and stones will break my bones, but names will never hurt me"? This story is so not true. Words have power. Our self-talk and talk to others have power. Therefore, it's our responsibility to monitor our internal self-chatter and what we say to others.

Through thinking and reflecting I realized that I had been making decisions based on emotions. For a long time, my emotions controlled me; I didn't control them. I acted on almost every impulse.

My first personal growth book that I allowed to plant a seed within me: Think and Grow Rich by Napoleon Hill

I was always reading books! I was thirsty for knowledge and wanted to feel healthy and happy mentally.

The first personal growth book I read was entitled *Think and Grow Rich* by Napoleon Hill. A page from that book that has never left my memory states that there is only one thing we can control in life and that is our thoughts. We either control them, or they control us.

I cannot express to you how powerful this statement was for me and my growth. Since that moment on I began working to strengthen my mind, select my thoughts, explore the power behind thoughts, and learn the processes of what makes the mind.

BIGGEST GAME CHANGEER OF MY LIFE!

Through these personal growth processes that I created for me I realized that I was searching for love. *I realized my inner superhero was searching for HOW TO BE THERE FOR ERICA.*

"I have gone from being suicidal to falling in love with life and me."

This process was when I really made a dent in maintaining my mental health strength. I can only speak for me; after the HIGH DAYS of the awakening my thought processes went back to habits. The good news is that I was NOW READY to deal with my inner pain.

"I used my inner superhero to BE with Erica (my inner villain)."

My inner superhero was stronger than ever. When I felt emotions of fear, sadness, and low energy I would use my inner superhero to comfort, support, and BE THERE for inner villain Erica.

As I promised in the beginning, I am not going to sugarcoat things. There were times when inner villain Erica wanted nothing to do with my inner superhero. She would resist my love and acceptance. In those moments, I would let her BE, I would accept those emotions and feelings, and accept and love her unconditionally. I would allow her to be her. I would let her know that I am not going anywhere and when she is ready to talk and to figure things out that I am here for her.

Persistence Pays OFF, ALWAYS!

I would keep this practice up and with time Erica began to open up to me. We began to build a strong healthy friendship. She would open up to me and show me why I was feeling hurt, angry, or resentful. She showed me some past memories that I was able to comfort and talk to (using my inner superhero).

MINDSET SHIFTING

I used a life changing technique that allowed me to work through the pain, ease the emotions I had experienced during these life events, and shift the way I was thinking about the events. I engage in what I call MINDSET SHIFTING. This is a technique of the inner superhero. What this means is you can feel multiple emotions at once. You can feel happy and you can feel sad all at the same time. The mission here is to feel and embrace all your emotions and choose to align with the emotion that will give you the outcome you want.

The power of acceptance

No matter what emotions you feel right now, I want you to honour them.

*** Note that this is a natural process and will differ from person to person. ***

As time went on, my inner villain and inner superhero started to become one again!

I am so happy and grateful for this process. My inner superhero had to fight and not give up when it was hard (sometimes I took breaks, but I would always go back to deal with my inner villain). This was a fight for my life of health and happiness. I had to invest the time into my health and keep focused on my end goal which was to integrate my inner villain and inner superhero as one again.

"This is an ongoing practice!"

Remember, life isn't perfect. Whenever I feel a wave of emotion that is challenging to deal with, I remember this technique and apply it right away. (more on this later in the How To Deal Section.)

The antidote to curing the inner villain's pain is self love.

I've learned that one of the most powerful antidotes is love. Love is the highest vibration frequency on this planet and can shift and move emotions around that are vibrating at a lower level. Being my own superhero was my cure. My inner superhero was searching to connect with my pain and deal with it. My inner superhero gave love to my inner pain; this began the process of healing and transformation.

If you aren't going to Love your Pain, who is?!

YOU'VE GOT THE POWER!

"BE THERE FOR YOUR INNER VILLAIN"

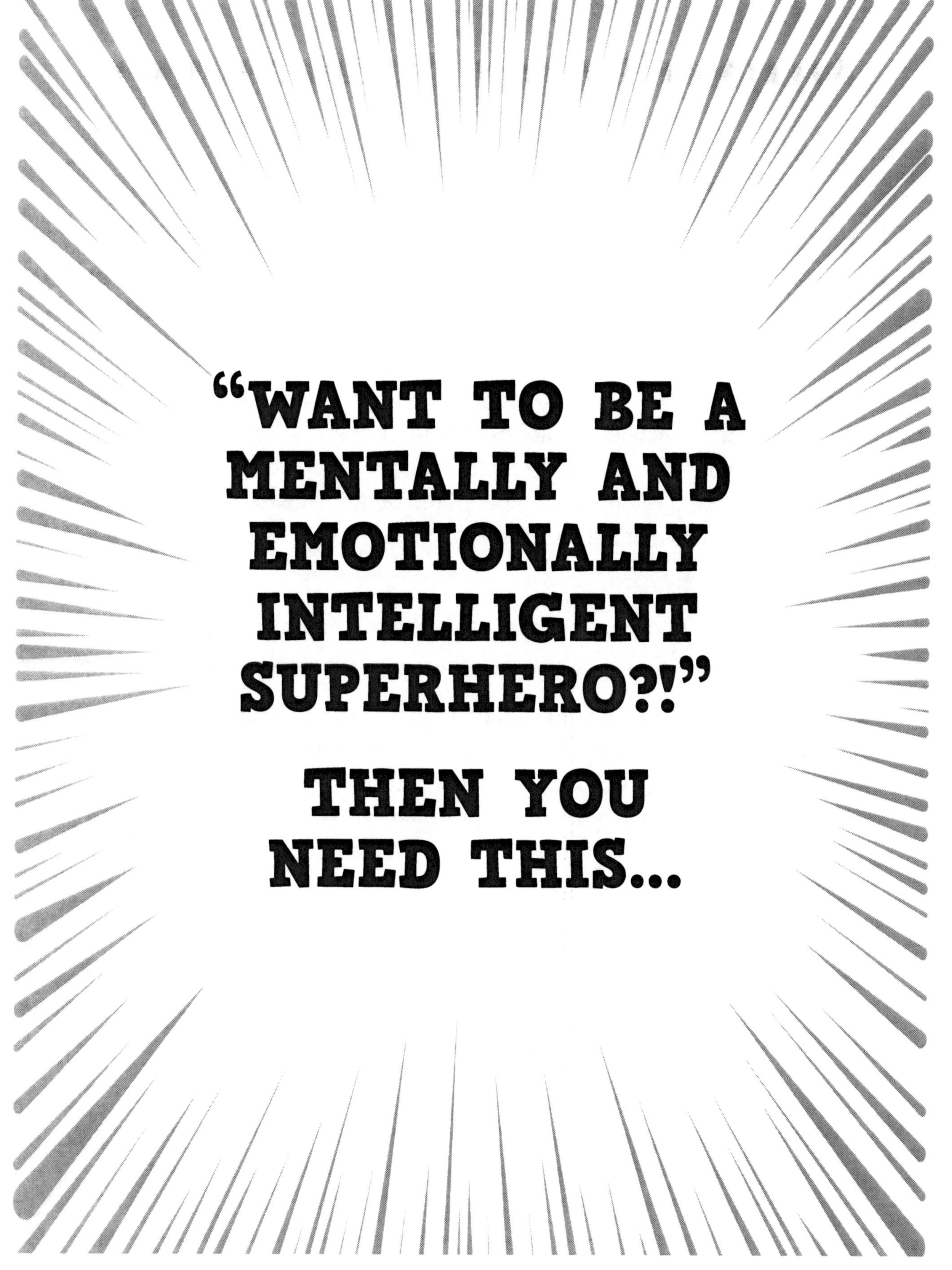
"WANT TO BE A MENTALLY AND EMOTIONALLY INTELLIGENT SUPERHERO?!"
THEN YOU NEED THIS...

Superhero Decision Making Formula

thoughts = feelings = where decisions are made
from (actions or behaviours) = outcomes

It was through meditation and waking up my inner superhero that I discovered the power behind what I call the Superhero Decision Making Formula.

I use this formula + How To Deal With Life Events (you will learn about this soon) before I make decisions. It has served me well with building friendships and family relationships, making tough business decisions, sticking to an exercise regime, building my skills by reading books, and attending courses and more. I am so excited to share this formula with you! ENJOY.

"My Inner Superhero used these Tools to save the rest of my school days and life!"

With this formula you will be able to power yourself up to overcome bullying and peer pressure; let go of other people's opinions of you; shift from negative thinking to positive thinking; enhance positive feelings; embrace your imperfections; go after goals and dreams such as a scholarship, award, job, or date; build new friendships; earn good grades; and go after whatever goal or plan you desire to achieve! The choice is up to you, my friend.

Remember, decisions have tremendous power. Our decisions determine our life outcomes. Our decisions always lead to a result. Your life course is a result of the decisions you make today.

Drum Roll please... Let me introduce you to the Superhero Decision Making Formula, and then we are going to do an exercise together to apply what we have learned. Sound awesome?

SUPERHERO DECISION MAKING FORMULA

Stop: This means you stop before taking action. You want to go through the following steps to ensure your actions are aligned with what you want your outcome to be.

Feel: What emotions do you feel at this moment? Emotions are like tidal waves. They go up and down and sometimes all around. They come and they go. Wait for the emotions to settle down so you can use your logic to assess the situation and your decision to move forward.

Think: Evaluate what your thoughts are. Thoughts come and go. Some thoughts are aligned with your inner superhero and some thoughts are aligned with pain. Learn to accept that all the thoughts are there in existence, and then choose to select your thoughts. On average, the human mind has over 20,000 thoughts per day.

Act: This is the step that has the most power. Action is the key to change. We cannot take back our actions.

Reflection: Reflection is one of the most practiced steps. Reflection is an important part of this process.

Superhero Decision Making Formula

Stop:

Feel:

Think:

Act:

Reflect:

printable sheets - www.ericahumphrey.com

I bet you have already naturally been engaged in the Superhero Decision Making Formula before!

Use this formula when you meditate for the best results!

I discovered this process after awakening my inner superhero through meditation to see what works and what doesn't. Meditation is about mindfulness, awareness, presence, and intelligence. I just LOVE meditation. This upcoming exercise is a form of meditation. Integrating meditation into your mental decision making process will serve you greatly and will enhance your mental health.

We have an internal self talk
happening...
talk about the power of
our internal story...

What's Your Story

(what is your self talk?)

When I woke up my inner superhero, I learned that there is an internal story playing in our mind from past events like a script, movie, or record playing over and over. This mental movie has power over our beliefs of our self and the world and the people in it and ultimately impacts our health, happiness, and success in life.

As you have seen in the real world, some movies can be inspiring, motivating, happy, funny, healthy, and adventurous or they can be sad, scary, or mysterious. The choice is yours in which movie you are going to watch.

The purpose of this section is to bring awareness to your mental story that is playing in your head. Once we are aware then we can focus on making some cuts or edits to our story of parts that are not serving you with greatness, because the power is within you to decide how your mental movie is going to play. Often in life we have got to make some changes in order to line ourselves up with our goals. This process is part of our life work.

You are the director of your life! What
characters are you playing out?

You, like the director of a play or movie, are the creator of your story. You have the opportunity and honour of changing the perception of your life events and turning the perceived challenges or liabilities into opportunities or assets. Have you ever been to a play or movie or event with a friend? Afterwards the two of you may have talked about your opinions of the event only to find out that you each had a completely different opinion even though you had been at the same event? Perception is a big deal in how we view the world.

In this section I want you to focus on identifying the story that you are telling yourself about your past and who you are today. Are you telling yourself that you're not worthy of love, health, happiness, or success? Or are you telling yourself how much you love you, how special you are, and how resilient you are? Do you laugh with yourself, etc.? I recommend doing this exercise once every three months to celebrate your growth and/or to work through internal challenges you are facing. Remember, life is not perfect and there is a reason and driving force behind what happens in your life. Trust life. Write to figure this all out. Empower yourself today by writing your life story now!

"Our story is never ending and constantly unfolding."

Writing my story has been and still is one of the biggest healing activities that I engage in!

Write Your Life Story Here

WOW! Amazing work! Congratulations; you just got to know yourself better. There is no right or wrong in writing your story. I am so happy that you have practice reflecting on your life story. Our opinion of ourselves is the most important opinion on this planet! You've got to LOVE who you are and know that you are the creator of your story! This is just the beginning for you :) The best is yet to come! I promise!

How to Deal with Life Events

"When life hands you lemons, make lemonade!"

A MENTAL BREAKTHROUGH

During my healing journey I experienced many breakthroughs. One of the key breakthroughs I learned is the power of thoughts. I learned that by changing the way I thought about a past life event I would feel different towards it. I practiced looking for the positives in past situations to release the pain, anger, and resentment I was carrying forward. Like training for a sport, the more I practiced the stronger my decision making muscles became. I was conditioning my thought patterns to look at the positive in people and life situations.

In this chapter I am going to share some examples of my life events in hopes of inspiring you to work through a life event that may be holding you back.

"I LET GO OF PLAYING THE BLAME GAME."

In the past, I rarely took responsibility for my actions. This was one of the reasons that I felt stuck in the past. It was always someone else's fault. I allowed my parents' actions to define me. I was acting out. What I didn't know then that I know now is that I was crying out for help. I was experiencing internal pain and didn't know how to deal with it. That pain is what inspired the How to Deal with Life Events worksheet. I decided to write out past life events and emotions that I didn't understand. I looked at why I was feeling a certain way about a past event to guide me through my healing and help me navigate through life. This process worked so well for me I decided to share it with others.

I created the Wheel of Life Game.

When I started speaking in schools, I wanted to create a FUN, engaging game for students that got the message across but also gave students the opportunity to experience building up their self esteem and confidence in a safe atmosphere. I wanted to create an atmosphere and program where students got the opportunity right then and there to do "the work" to develop the muscles of self esteem and confidence to overcome school and life challenges. This is when the Wheel of Life Game was born.

This game builds confidence in real time!

What makes this game powerful is that students are given the opportunity to practice using their decision making muscles to make decisions in real time that they will have to face in their lives at some point in a safe, fun, and respectful atmosphere. In addition, students learn that they are powerful enough to overcome a past life event that is still negatively impacting their lives.

"I am all about making life fun, especially the life work we are required to embark on. I have always loved games and felt inspired to create a game out of HOW TO DEAL with life events."

By sharing some of my stories and life events that I have grown through, I hope that they will inspire you to work through some of your own life challenges. I challenge you to write down some of your life events as well and work through them.

It is our story, our inner self talk, and our opinion of perceived events that are linked to our internal suffering. How we view an event is important. Our story about the event is either linked to our past pain or our life wisdom that we can use in our toolkit today.

Erica's Examples of How to Deal With Life Events

Life Event: Parents' Separation

Past Thought Pattern:

I thought that there was something wrong with me. I thought that I wasn't worthy of love, health, or happiness because my parents weren't together.

Today's Thought Pattern:
My parents' separation and divorce wasn't personal to me. What they were going through together was about them. I have since learned the life lessons of how important communication is and of how to separate myself from someone else's life challenges. I have learned the importance of taking time before making big life decisions like pregnancy and marriage to make sure I choose the right person to build a life together with.

Life Event: Traumatic separation where my dad influenced me to come live with him. This event caused my mom to become upset and resulted in me living with my dad, away from my mom and brothers.

Past Thought Pattern:
I trusted my dad and liked what I heard from him. He asked me to live with him which made me feel loved. I truly felt like I would be able to share my time by living with both my dad and my mom, but the events didn't turn out that way.

Today's Thought Pattern:
I forgive my dad for his pain and suffering. I know he was upset and hurt. He was using his inner villain to make decisions that caused pain to others. Today I know I have my inner superhero to stand up and protect me against other people's pain through my superpowers of communication skills and positive thinking. I know how to release my pain in healing ways such as fitness and outdoor activities.

Life Event: Peer Pressure to smoke cigarettes!

Past Thought Pattern:
When influenced by peer pressure to start smoking, I agreed, even though a piece inside me didn't want to. I was fearful to say no because I thought that I would lose friends. What I didn't know then that I know now is if a person didn't want to be my friend because

I said no to smoking, then they weren't really my friend in the first place. Looking back I didn't trust life to bring me the friends in my life who would honour my decisions and be good healthy influences.

Today's Thought Pattern: Peer or Societal Pressure
I have learned how to build self esteem and confidence to overcome life pressures and challenges. I have learned to trust my inner superhero. I have learned to trust that inner conscience to say no to influences that are not aligned with who I am and my life purpose. I trust life and know that the right people will show up at the right time in life. I choose to put myself in healthy environments to attract awesome friends!

Life Event: Arrested and sent into custody

Past Thought Pattern:
I was too scared to choose differently and move away from peer pressure. I was a follower and not a leader. I was angry and thought some attention from my parents was better than no attention. I thought I was being cool. Once I was already in trouble I felt like I was beyond the place of return. I thought I was worthless and that nobody would like me.

Today's Thought Pattern:
I forgave myself for past events and learned that the past does not dictate my future. I began to hear my inner superhero and listened to thoughts of love, success, forgiveness, and peace. I have realized that sometimes we get lost before we get found.

Life Event: Suicide attempt

Past Thought Pattern:
I felt so sad, worthless, and lonely. I thought no one would miss me if I died. I felt so much pain that I couldn't see another way out. The truth is my inner superhero didn't want me to go... but my inner villain's thought process was more powerful!

Today's Thought Pattern:

I know that I am born for a purpose. I know that life has a plan for me. I trust the natural process of life and I trust that people and life events come into my life for a purpose of growth. I choose to go with the flow of life.

Life Event: Dad dropped me off at CAS

Past Thought Pattern:
I thought that if my dad didn't want me then I must not be any good or loveable. I thought something was wrong with me. I thought that I must be worthless and pathetic.

Today's Thought Pattern:
I realized that my dad felt powerless and didn't know how to parent. I have learned not to allow people's actions to affect me in a negative way. I have worked through the pain of abandonment. I am worthy, healthy, happy, and valuable to many human beings.

Life Event: Enter rehab in Thunder Bay

Past Thought Pattern:
I felt dependant on substances. I had learned to use substances to deal with my emotions, regardless of the pain that these substances caused to my mind, body, and soul.

Today's Thought Pattern:
I am aware of my emotions and have created healthy channels to release my emotions including communication skills. I know that if I cover up an emotion then the emotion will still be there. For me to deal with my emotions I have to get real with myself and I have the power to do so.

Life Event: Being kicked out of my dad's house with nowhere to go

Past Thought Pattern:
I was scared, lost, and confused. I didn't know what I would do or where I would live. I felt the pain of not feeling loved. I felt worthless and alone. I was fearful because I was sleeping at different unhealthy

places every night. I remember experiencing women's health issues and struggling to find help.

Today's Thought Pattern:
I know I have the personal power to solve any life problem. Anything is possible. When life events throw me for a loop, I choose to look for the solutions and the positive pieces. If there is a will there is a way.

Put this into Action

Use your Superhero Decision Making Formula and find a quite place for you to reflect. Write out your own life events and how to deal with them.

How to Deal with Life Events

Life Event:

How do you perceive the event today?

____

____

____

____

What activities can you do to release how you feel in a constructive way?

____

____

____

____

How can you think about this life event differently so that you can feel differently?

____

____

____

____

Life Event:

How do you perceive the event today?

____

____

____

____

What activities can you do to release your feelings in a constructive way?

____

____

____

____

How can you look at the event differently so that you feel differently?

____

____

____

____

Life Event:

How do you perceive the event today?

____

____

____

____

What activities can you do to release how you feel in a constructive way?

____

____

____

____

How can you look at the event differently so that you feel differently?

____

____

____

____

Life Event:

How do you perceive the event today?

What activities can you do to release how you feel in a constructive way?

How can you look at the event differently so that you feel differently?

Emotional Intelligence

Sometimes we don't know where our emotions are coming from, and therefore we may not know how to deal. That is okay. Trust that you are not alone.

What emotions are you feeling lately?

____

____

____

____

Where do you think these emotions are coming from?

____

____

____

____

When you feel these emotions, how do you deal with them? What actions do you take? For example, do you talk to someone, engage in a fitness activity, meditate, etc.?

____

____

____

____

What emotions are you feeling lately?

Where do you think these emotions are coming from?

When you feel these emotions, how do you deal with them? What actions do you take?

What emotions are you feeling lately?

Where do you think these emotions are coming from?

____

____

____

____

When you feel these emotions, how do you deal with them? What actions do you take?

____

____

____

____

You can download more how to deal sheets at

www.ericahumphrey.com

You are doing amazing work! Congrats. It is time to move on to the next level of awesomeness :) Remember, these topics are in a specific order for a reason as they have been designed to empower you to experience an amazing life change. I am so excited to share the next piece of the building block to awaken your inner superhero.

YOU ARE AMAZING!!!

"WHAT ARE YOUR NATURAL TALENTS, GIFTS, ABILITIES, PASSIONS, AND SKILLS? HOW DO YOU USE THESE SUPERPOWERS TO BUILD RELATIONSHIPS IN YOUR LIFE?"

Superpower, Relationship Building, and Character Development

How Igniting your Superhero's Superpowers will open the door for your Inner Superhero and guide you to build the best relationships in your life!

"When you know yourself you are empowered. When you accept yourself you are invincible."

- Tina Lifford

In this chapter we are going to identify, highlight, and focus on your natural talents, gifts, abilities, passions, and skills (which I call your superpowers) through recognizing and developing your superhero superpowers.

This exercise is both fun and cool because you will discover and uncover knowing who you are and what you have to offer which will build self esteem and confidence. This new understanding will not only strengthen your relationship with yourself, but with others.

I truly believe a large part of our happiness in life is the result of the type of relationships and quality of relationships in our lives. I will shed light onto the different levels of relationships and explain why they are each important.

You will be using the previous Inner Superhero building blocks to be a catalyst in working through the next sections. You will see the power in using your superhero decision making formula, being aware of your story about who you are, plus the how to deal with life events to build relationships with others.

My mission here is for you to develop the healthiest and happiest relationships in life by using your natural born superpowers and getting real with your people!

What are Superpowers?

Every human being has natural talents and gifts. I believe that these gifts or superpowers are aligned with each person's life purpose. Identifying my superpowers was a piece of the puzzle that led to the awakening of my inner superhero.

How do you know what your natural talents, gifts, abilities, and skills are? Well, ask yourself what activities you do that just sing to your soul. What activities do you do that bring you so much energy and positivity that you feel alive and passionate? What activities do you do that are effortless for you? What activities bring a smile to your face, or make you light up like a light bulb? What activities bring you joy, fun, laughter, and happiness?!

Some of our superpowers need some development and strength. Our superhero superpowers are always within us, but sometimes we get distracted or lost in life and we don't use them. Sometimes people use them for personal gain despite how their actions directly or indirectly impact others. Regardless of the situation, these superpowers can be powered up to FULL FORCE to save your day and build the life of your dreams! That is what this section is all about.

Time to Unleash your Superpowers!

In this section, I am going to share with you my superpowers and ask you to write out yours :) I use these powers to live a healthy and happy life. I cannot emphasize enough the power of recognizing my natural talents, gifts, abilities, and skills. Choosing to align with my natural born superpowers awoke my inner superhero and saved my life. We are going to identify your natural born superpowers to awaken your inner superhero - that is what it takes! It was the awakening and developing of these superpowers that allowed me to overcome my fears, doubts, and worries so that I could push my way through to success.

Get Excited because Greatness is about to be unleashed!

Allow me to share some of my superpowers!

My Superpower of Faith / Intuition / Trusting the process of life

I wouldn't be where I am today without igniting my faith and allowing it to grow. Having faith in something greater and believing that anything is possible is what got me through the tough times when life seemed so dark. I heavily relied on my intuition (and still do to this day) to recognize and follow my inner compass or guidance system in making decisions and taking action steps towards goals and dreams. If I don't get an opportunity or something that I want, I trust that there is a purpose to this. Or on the flip side, if something arrives on my plate like school work, personal growth activities, or work for a company, I trust that there is a reason for it and look for those answers. I trust the natural process of life. This is part of my inner superhero. Today, my faith and intuition are so strong. I always rely on my intuition in what I feel inspired to do, then I count on my superhero decision making formula and how to deal sheets if needed. I use this superpower to go after my goals and dreams too! Sometimes we just know this without explanation and that is what I call faith and intuition.

My Superpower of Fitness

I was born with fitness in my blood. It was my superpower from a very young age and fitness runs in my family. In my early childhood years, I participated in track and field events, skating, hockey, and baseball. As you know, I started teaching fitness and healthy living at a very young age. Through my passion for fitness I have been able to inspire others to create healthy and fit lifestyles. Fitness is my drug; it is my happy place :) Practicing fitness has and does allow me to achieve high levels of happiness and success.

My Superpower of Confidence

I have used the power of confidence to land me job interviews, attend life building courses and seminars, have tough conversations with people to ensure healthy boundaries were set, make tough decisions on what friends I want in my life, travel, build a business, network, and try new life skills and experiences. Confidence has allowed me to be a strong leader who inspires change in others' lives. I am confident not just in my own abilities but in the abilities of others as well.

My Superpower of Positive Thinking

Learning how to focus on the positive of a situation is a MASSIVE superpower for me in my life. Through trial and error, I have learned how focusing on the positive manifests more positive in my life. I specifically learned this when I was working in counseling to heal from my view of my parents. When I spend time with my parents I focus on the bright side of them and allow their negative to be. Applying this superpower has allowed me to strengthen healthy relationships with my parents. After all, life can be challenging. I believe in growth, forgiveness, being the leader, and acceptance.

Super Power of Courage

Being a fearless leader to create the life I desire is a power that I believe everyone has inside of themselves. To be clear here, this doesn't mean that I don't feel fear. This means that I feel fear and move forward anyways. I have learned how to use fear to empower me vs. paralyze me. I have found the courage to leave unhealthy relationships, friendships, and work environments and to reach for dreams like travel, business awards, and scholarships! This superpower comes to me naturally. I love feeling happy and healthy – it is just more fun! I have used this superpower to get me through the challenging days. This superpower is also a relationship builder of excitement.

My Superpower of Resiliency

"I've strength in these muscles to jump up faster than ever before!" When I think of resiliency I think of one of my favourite movie series - *Rocky*. My dad and I still watch this series from time to time. Rocky's personal story is powerful. One of my favourite quotations is that it is not how often you get knocked down, it is about how you get back up on your feet. I have failed many times in life because life is learning. Sometimes as human beings it takes a few times of falling down to learn the life lesson. The beautiful truth is that there is nothing in life that we can't overcome and achieve. I am so dedicated and focused on my mission that no matter how many times I get knocked down, I will get back up. This superpower worked to awaken my inner superpower. I apply this technique in all aspects of my life through fitness, relationships, writing this book :), and MORE!

My Superpower of Asking for Help

Nothing great was ever accomplished by one person. If we were meant to do everything on our own, then we could live on a planet by ourselves. The truth is that we are meant to connect, grow, and develop relationships with people on this planet. When I look back on how I grew through my growing pains to achieve my goals, I see that I was assisted by working with others. I asked for help when I needed it, and I worked with other people's superpowers to achieve a common goal! Through asking for help I was able to attend rehab and begin the process of working through my addictions. I found the group home when my commitment shifted me to another direction. I created a social justice group dedicated to serving others. I won a business scholarship award, started a speaking business, and MORE! I challenge you to ask for help today! It is a STRENGTH to ask for help, not a weakness!

My Superpower of Imperfection

When I learned that perfection doesn't exist, this realization literally strengthened the bond of love within myself and toward others.

This superpower ties into being a student of life. You see, no one or no one situation is perfect in life. I joke that the only way to see things perfectly is through seeing our imperfections as perfect, because this is the truth. Life is not "perfect". I don't know exactly where we learn to seek perfection from. Regardless, I have not let the idea of perfection stop me from achieving my goals and dreams. This has been life changing.

My Superpower of Not Taking Things Personally

This was a big life changer for me. I now know and understand that every human being whether child, teen, sibling, or adult has their own personal experiences that they are speaking from. This is human nature. Every human being has created their own inner world and it is from those experiences that they are speaking from. Learning not to take my parents' separation or other people's behaviours personally granted me the freedom to break free from the negative thoughts I had surrounding the situation. I was able to continue taking steps forward on my missions regardless of other people's opinions, actions, or behaviours.

Self Esteem, LOVE, and Confidence Superpowers

If I could boil down a life change to one key ingredient that saves the lives of others, it would be self esteem. To me self esteem is the most powerful currency in the world. Self esteem is so powerful that it can save lives and change the quality of people's lives. That's what self esteem did for me, and I've seen it save the lives of others. Self esteem has the power to transform lives and the power to heal all wounds. I've witnessed self esteem heal depression, anxiety, suicidal thoughts, and inner pain. I've seen self esteem enhance and magnify the qualities within human beings: beautiful qualities of self-love, self worth, confidence, worthiness, and respect. These high level/ feel good energies have the power to shift the direction and course of people's lives into alignment with love, wealth, health, abundance, peace, and personal empowerment. This alignment connects the mind, body, and soul so that you feel healthy and happy. I've seen love have the power to heal broken relationships on all levels of living, such as the relationship with self, life partners, families, friendships, colleagues, work situations, and overall relationships with everyday life and everyday people in the community. Simply put, love is powerful!

Superpower of Empowering the Inner Superheroes of Others

It just feels so good to serve others. Through empowering others, you create a mutual place of respect, honour, love, strength, purpose, etc. I could go on and on :) The truth is when we empower others we empower ourselves. Through this process we are developing ourselves and the leadership within the person we are empowering. It is a beautiful relationship that coexists between the two parties. I have used this technique countless times with fitness coaching and instructing, life coaching, and speaking. In my opinion, empowering others to succeed is truly the best way to teach life lessons.

Superpower of Making Stuff Happen!

I have learned how to make stuff happen in life and fast. I had to learn this superpower originally to survive in life. For example, when I was kicked out of my house and when I felt suicidal I had to find the answers to keep alive. I've been able to use this superpower to thrive in life. I used this skill to land me a business scholarship, to teach others fitness, and to create a healthy lifestyle for me to live independently on my own.

Superpower of Speaking My Truth!

This superpower led to my awakening. I had to bring light to my dark side to experience freedom and to live a healthy and happy life. I have since passed on this truth through working with others and it has served myself and others well.

Superpower of Listening

I want you to think back to a time when someone really listened to you. How did that make you feel? When people truly listen to others like there is nothing else going on in the world, they feel important and special. Listening to others with your mind, heart, and soul signifies leadership. I love using this superpower because people will just adore you and it personally feels good to give people the respect they deserve! I challenge you to listen fully with your peeps and see how they respond. In my opinion, listening is by far one of the greatest life gifts anyone can receive and give. Are you listening?

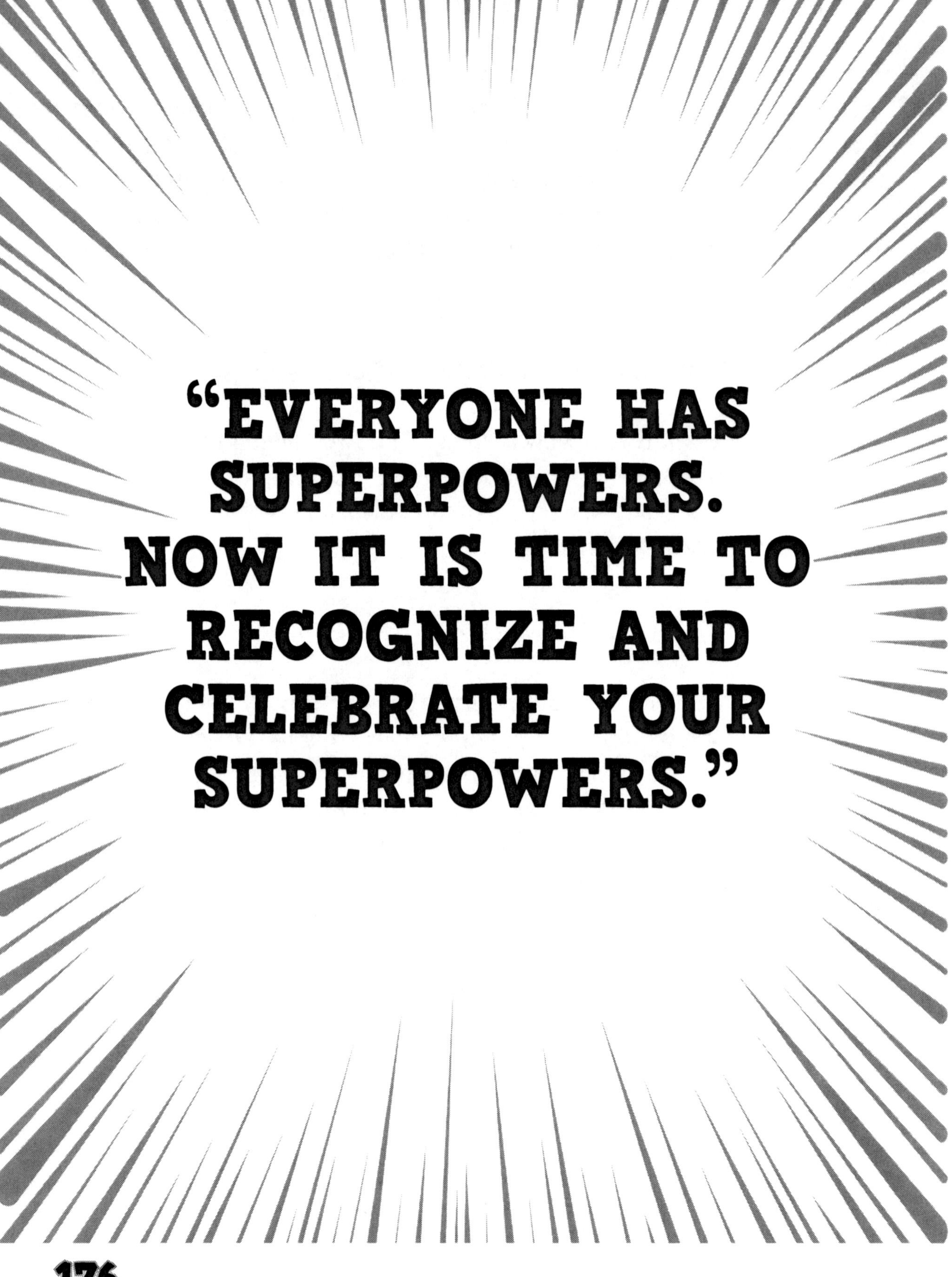

"EVERYONE HAS SUPERPOWERS. NOW IT IS TIME TO RECOGNIZE AND CELEBRATE YOUR SUPERPOWERS."

Being able to recognize and celebrate your very own unique talents, gifts, abilities, and skills is a sign that you possess a good level of self confidence and self esteem. During the next section, I want you to feel proud and happy by uncovering your amazing qualities and superpowers. I want you to unleash your great superpowers in this workbook while you honour and focus on your positive attributes.

Examples of Superpowers

courage
strength
vulnerability
mental intelligence
emotional intelligence
self awareness
kindness
ambition
commitment
loyalty
reliability
responsibility
respect
continuous learning
candour
authenticity
compassion
confidence
consistency
creativity
determination
faith
flexibility
friendship
goal-oriented
greatness
honesty
integrity
leadership
obedience
optimism

What are your Superpowers? Describe their power below

Superpower of

Superpower of

Superpower of

Superpower of

Superpower of

Superpower of

Superpower of

Superpower of

Superpower of

Superpower of

Superpower of

Go to www.ericahumphrey.com for more printable sheets.

Areas of Opportunities

As we discussed, perfection doesn't exist. I truly believe that life is designed for us to grow. What does that mean? To me it means that we are destined to release and unleash our inner superhero or greatness. Sometimes in order to do that we must focus on clearing up some of our inner baggage that prevents us from moving forward in our lives. In this section, I want you to focus on areas that you want to make a difference in your life. I challenge you to be gentle, real, and focused so you can turn these areas into superpowers!

Character Development Opportunity is Patience

I've got to say that out of all my super powers, patience has been the toughest one for me to learn and to be honest I am still learning it! I was always that kid who couldn't wait for trips or holidays. What I learned is that some things just take time. Learning how to be patient has served me well in my life journey of overcoming addictions, abuse, and bullying and of developing unconditional love for myself and others.

How can I deal with this? I can turn this into a superpower by...

I turned this into a superpower by first recognizing that I had some life work to do in this area. Next, I choose to be aware that when I felt uneasy it was usually because I felt impatient. Through trusting and respecting the process of life and letting go of control, I have been able to enhance my patience. I have learned that there are times to get things done, and this is where I can let go of patience. This has helped me get results in business. I have learned through trial and error and by asking questions.

Character Development Opportunity is Being
the Change I Wanted to See.

This superpower took me some time to ignite. I would take a step forward, and then a couple of steps back. A couple of steps forward, and then a step back. Igniting this superpower allowed me to work through some of my hurt, anger, and resentment toward others. I had always heard the words "be the change you want to see in the world." These words made sense to me. I knew these words had power, but they didn't really hit me until I woke up my own inner superhero. I realized that allowing my thoughts, feelings, and behaviours to be aligned with what I wanted to see in someone else actually produced the results I was looking for. For example, when someone I knew was being mean to me, instead of being mean back I showed love. It was amazing to watch his reaction. He turned around and gave so much love back to me. I love using this superpower because I can take negativity and turn it into positive! SO POWERFUL!

How can I deal with this? I can turn this into a superpower by...

I am going to keep this one simple. I wanted to see change in the world and in people, and I knew that I had to be the leader in that change - no matter what!

Character Development Opportunity is...

How can I deal with this? I can turn this into a superpower by...

Character Development Opportunity is...

How can I deal with this? I can turn this into a superpower by...

Character Development Opportunity is...

____

How can I deal with this? I can turn this into a superpower by...

Character Development Opportunity is...

How can I deal with this? I can turn this into a superpower by...

"THE BEST RELATIONSHIP YOU WILL EVER HAVE IN YOUR LIFE IS WITH YOU."

Life is Relationships

I am extremely excited to share with you the relationship formula I created to take my life from surviving to thriving.

Through awakening my inner superhero I discovered there is a hierarchy of relationships that lead to greatness!

Discovering the power of relationships was key to my personal happiness that led to mountains of change in my life!

I discovered that not only are relationships important, but there is a specific hierarchy in creating strong, lasting, fulfilling, and healthy relationships. I learned this through awakening my inner superhero. The strong relationship I have developed with my inner superhero has shown me the path of healthy living.

When I think of relationships I think of having a relationship with life, a belief in something greater which some call faith. I think of the relationships with myself, my life purpose, work partnerships; I think of family; and most definitely I think of the community in which we live. This section is dedicated to the relationships described above in that order.

Growing through the school days my relationship priority was out of order. I used to put people I barely knew in order of importance before me, my family, and my friends. As a result, I broke some relationships because they sensed their lack of importance. I had to rebuild relationships throughout all levels of life. I learned, created, and implemented an order of relationships to create a healthy lifestyle. This hierarchy is based on personal empowerment, independence, and healthy living. I am so excited to share this with you!

First, let's recognize what a relationship is. A relationship is the way in which two or more concepts, objects, or people are connected, or the state of being connected.

In my opinion, the next level of a relationship is the type of connection. When you connect with you or someone else do you connect on a deep level, or is it only on a surface level? For example, when you meet someone do you speak your truth? Do you ask real questions about who they are and where they are at in their life, or do you only ask about surface stuff like materials, physique, what job they have, etc.?

Let's Make Relationships Real!

If I had to boil down one word to describe relationships it would be CONNECTION. We must feel connected to ourselves and to others to feel involved in society and to feel a part of something greater which is what we are all looking for. We need to have faith in others and in ourselves.

To feel important, connected, and special is our birthright!

I truly believe that every single person is looking to belong, to feel connected, and to feel a part of something greater than themselves. I believe this is part of honouring who we are.

Through failing, falling down, making mistakes, and understanding what solutions worked and what didn't I established a hierarchical order of relationships that has fulfilled me, my life, and the people in it. I share with you these stories to inspire you to live a life full of healthy, happy, loving relationships!

"Through the process of personal growth I realized that the first relationship in life was with me and faith in a higher power."

During my school years I felt so lost and confused. I felt disconnected from myself, my family, my friends, my school, my work, and my community and I had a low sense of faith - I lacked a belief in anything larger than myself.

"I was looking on the outside to solve my issues on the inside."

I was searching on the outside of myself to find solutions. For example, I was using drugs to soothe the inner pain I experienced.

I was looking for a relationship to feel love. I was looking for a boy to solve my inner issues. These tactics didn't work - long term. They were only short term solutions.

"I had to put a belief in something greater than myself and human existence. I call this faith! I believe that there is something greater out there watching over us all, and so I leaned on my faith for guidance!"

What worked long term was putting my wants, needs, and desires out to life/the universe/higher-power/God/Allah/whoever or whatever you want to call source. I completely surrendered and told God that I would do whatever it took to find peace, rest, and inner grace. I asked and I did receive! Asking for guidance lead my higher power to respect that I was ready for guidance in life. This process led to awakening and connecting with my inner superhero.

Ultimately, my inner superhero saved my relationship with me! My inner superhero stood up to my inner fears, insecurities, and pain within through strength, courage, truth, and tough/unconditional love.

In growing through my growing pains, I realized that I had lost a connection with myself along the way - or perhaps I hadn't connected with my true authentic self yet. When I woke up my inner superhero I realized that the missing piece was me. I realized that I needed to strengthen and develop my relationship with me. This needed to happen first and foremost, because I had lost a connection with myself. I realized that I am born by myself. I enter and exit this planet by myself, and so I must be naturally designed to solve my own needs.

"I had to look on the inside to fill the inner whole."

Once I realized that I had the power to fill my own inner whole, I began to live life differently. I began to take care of myself physically, emotionally, mentally, and spiritually. I became best friends with me. I was honest with me and stopped hiding behind my pain. When I experienced negative thinking, sadness, anxiety, fear, or depression, I remembered that I needed to be there for me. I needed to support myself emotionally, mentally, and spiritually. Erica needed to be there for Erica!

I stopped running away from myself and started being the person I was looking for others to be.

For the longest time before my awakening, I was running away from myself. I was running away from my inner pain. I didn't want to face it, and so I suppressed the emotions. I was running away from a relationship with me.

When my inner superhero emerged, I naturally knew how to tap into my superpowers to discover and learn how to heal. I learned how to release the negative thinking and I understood more about these emotions and where they were coming from. I began to develop a strong, beautiful relationship with me. My pains and hurts began to open up to me (my inner superhero), to allow me to support my pain. This processes unfolded naturally as I began to trust myself and life. I began to understand that a lot of negativity had come from my childhood. I had pain over childhood events that had happened which I had no control over. The only control I had was to begin to look at these events differently to feel differently. This process was about integrating my negative thoughts into positive ones. I began to love me unconditionally. I began to love my pain and forgive my pain. I learned what unconditional love was because I saw that my behaviours and actions were created out of desperation for love, attention, affection, connection, feeling important, etc. I began to forgive myself for the past choices and decisions I had made. I saw clearly that I was passing down the pain I was feeling that I hadn't cleared up yet. I realized that my pain and suffering were negatively affecting my relationships with myself and others. I realized that I had been running for me, running from the truth, running from dealing with my pain for so long, simply because I wasn't aware of the truth or had the knowledge of how to grow through the pain. I had to grow through the pain by connecting with me - Erica.

"The best relationship you will ever have in life is with you."

The first relationship in the hierarchy is a relationship with you! I learned in life that no one can make me happy but me. I realized that no one else can take better care of me but me! I kept looking outside of myself for someone or something else to fill the inner whole within that lacked love, self esteem, confidence, etc. But at the end of the day, I was looking for ME to stand up and be my own superhero!

To take care of you, you could attend a fitness class. Choose a couple of fitness classes that you are interested in. I like to take classes based on what people have recommended. Feel free to do a Google search.

You could also attend a workshop or seminar on a topic that you want to grow your knowledge in.

When I was rebuilding my life education, I began searching for topics such as real estate, motivation, and fitness. I kept my eye on the lookout for these topics. Find a seminar in your local area on a topic that you want to learn more about and attend it!

Self Discovery

Mirror Work Part 1

Mirror Work is extremely powerful. This type of mirror work is when you look at you in the mirror. You take this opportunity to focus on the areas that you love about you! Take inventory of areas that you feel need enhanced love. Write them down and practice sending love to these areas. Know that no one or one thing is perfect in life.

Mirror Work Part 2

Level 2 is advanced. When I say advanced I mean that human beings need a level of emotional and spiritual intelligence. I have used this technique to facilitate my transformation and transcendence to building my self esteem and confidence. It goes like this: you may notice something you don't like in someone else. For example, you may notice that someone is being rude, loud, annoying, angry, etc. This often is a reflection of something you don't like within you that you haven't dealt with yet. So when I notice there is something that I don't appreciate in someone, I ask myself, is there something within me that needs attention? Is there a quality within me that requires healing? I use this experience as an opportunity to facilitate change and progression in my life journey. It works like a charm!

Remember, you've got to be open to it. If these qualities exist within, ignoring them doesn't dissolve them: they are still there. Rather, let's be the fearless leader and SUPERHERO for ourselves to work through our inner resistance and pain. Let's clear ourselves up so we can live the life of our dreams! The hard work only feels hard in the beginning, and this varies depending on the individual. Before you know it you will be on this amazing path and journey of realizing your true potential, authentic self, and life's purpose. Unleash your journey!

It is so worth the work and one day you will feel free, clean, and clear. SO WORTH IT!

Stand Up and Be Your Own Superhero!

TODAY IS THE DAY!

Life Purpose/Career/ Work Relationships

The next type of relationship in the hierarchy is life purpose/career/ work relationships. I put this type as number two because as human beings we spend a lot of our time working. In my opinion, there is a strong sense of self esteem and confidence in financially being able to support oneself through work that you LOVE!

Earning income is powerful in building our self esteem and confidence because we can care for ourselves and make independent decisions in life. Watching my mom struggle because she didn't have enough money to go out and build her own life was hard. My mom has inspired me to be financially independent and create my own lifestyle the way I want it, on my terms.

As students you have a fantastic opportunity to gain valuable life/ work experience through your volunteer hours. Take advantage of these hours. Employers look for experience on your resume. What better way for you to learn more about who you are and what future educational program you want to enter into than by being actively involved in choosing your volunteer experience! Carefully choose where you are going to spend your volunteer hours. This is a smart way to build skills and experience and see what you like and what you don't like. Who knows where it will take you :)

"Seize the opportunity of your volunteer hours in school and make the most of them!"

Remember when I went to go live in the group home? During this period I volunteered at various places such as Sister's Place, John Labatt Centre to raise funds for kids in Haiti who needed the basic necessities of life. I took on working assignments through which I grew and learned more about who I am and what I love to do.

These are the years to start that process of discovering who you are. Seize the opportunity and make the most of what is in front of you. Go find your passion in life!

Working in School?

Students ask me all the time about gaining their first job! I know some students and parents feel differently about this topic. I am aware that some students work for various reasons and as well as some students focus 100% on their grades. Personally, I don't think there is a right or wrong decision here. I think that the decision is dependent on the individual, their learning style, and their life plan. I recommend using the resources around you to make good decisions. For example, draw upon resources like your parents, teachers, guidance counselors, social workers, etc. Speak up and ask questions that are going to affect your future, because no one can better advocate for you than you! :)

Time Management Tips

Time management skills - there are 168 hours in the week. How do you use these hours to your benefit? What type of time management system or schedule do you have? How do you prioritize what is important to you? I recommend leaning on mentors, coaches, parents, and teachers - these are people who have really honed in on this skill! This is what I have done and it has served me well. Personally I link up my calendar to my phone and I use my email. I can easily schedule in my to do list and schedule reminders. I challenge you to find a system that works well for you, school, and life!

LET'S GET
REAL!

Family Relationships

The closest people we have in our lives are our family members. Think about it: our parents have known us the longest. In this section, I am going to share some stories on how I rebuilt a relationship with my family in hopes these stories will inspire you or someone you know.

My family's health and happiness dramatically suffered from the multiple separations, abuse, drama, divorce, court processes, and my detention centre admittance among other life events. I felt so isolated from my family. It took time to rebuild these relationships, and it is a lifelong process. I am going to share with you some insights on how I rebuilt relationships with my family. I want to be clear: although my family and I created many positive memories together, the negative seemed to outweigh the positive.

My family members had their own personal growth to complete.

First, I had to recognize that my parents aren't perfect. No one is. My parents had their own fears, pains, insecurities, hopes, and dreams too. I had to understand that life was not all about me. I had to realize that I was looking at real human beings who aren't perfect. When people are living in pain, it is challenging for them to be present and be there for their children because they need to grow physically, emotionally, mentally, and spirituality.

Personally, I have found my family relationships to be the most challenging relationships in my life. There was a time that I had to make a choice to decide if I wanted to be a part of my family or if I did not want to be involved in their lives.

I had to divorce my family.

There were periods of time where I left my family because I couldn't continue my growth while living in the same household. I had to protect myself and go live my life to continue my personal and professional growth. Although this was a hard decision, it was necessary. After I graduated the group home, I went to live on my own.

Every Person Has Positive Qualities (inner villain and inner superhero)

For a long time, I used to blame my parents and held emotions of anger and resentment toward them. It wasn't until I learned the POWER of ATTENTION that I was able to clear out those emotions (that were negatively affecting me). Through awakening my inner superhero, I realized that everyone has positive qualities. I then chose to focus on my parents' positive qualities - this focus actually brought out more of their positive qualities. I realized that my parents were engaged more with their inner villains, but their inner superheroes were there too. It wasn't their fault; they hadn't awakened their inner superheroes yet! I truly believe they didn't know how to awaken their inner superhero. My mission with my parents has been to lead by example and lead by change. I have been teaching my parents to awaken their inner superhero ever since.

After some time away and some healing, I decided I wanted my family back in my life. So I proposed to my mom and dad and asked to build relationships with them. I set clear boundaries with them. One was I wouldn't be around my dad when he was drinking. Another was that I needed my mom to stop treating me like my past; I needed her to treat me like a new person with a clean slate.

It was like my mom and I met for the first time. This was a process and took time, as nothing in life is perfect. It took communication, forgiveness, honesty, and love with one another. This process has been one of the most rewarding processes in my life. My relationship with my mom is the strongest it has ever been. I am so happy we have agreed to work together to create happiness memories together by moving forward. I LOVE YOU MOM!

My dad has struggled with hearing my story and moving forward. He is making progress today but still has a hard time talking about past events. I respect his space and his timing. I have learned to love and accept him for where he is at in his life. I was able to have "conversations" with my dad and share my feelings through journaling, drawing, painting, and fitness and through asking him questions about his childhood to understand his upbringing and where he came from. Learning this information allowed me to better understand my father's behaviour and mindset.

Forgiveness is a process.

My healing and forgiveness of my childhood has been a process of realizing that every negative behaviour has a positive intention behind it. I truly believe that my parents did the best they could to raise us kids. I mean there is no book on how to live life, is there? We often pass down ways of living based on what we have been passed down. I am happy to report that my parents and I have a great relationship today.

* Choosing to be a part of my family was a personal decision. I believe so strongly in forgiveness. I believe that people do the best they can with the knowledge and resources they have. I forgave my parents and started to see the positives. I began to teach my parents how to forgive, love themselves, accept past events, and find the beauty in life through living by example.

"Tips on How I Continue to Build and Strengthen a Relationship with my Family"

* I began to see our similarities.

* We often are the sum of our parents. I accepted that some things that I don't like within them may be qualities within me that I do not like as well. For example, my father didn't follow through on his commitments which upset me. Later I realized that I was behaving that way as well. I would then practice self reflection with meditation and the superstar decision making formula. I used my feelings of frustrations with my parents as an opportunity for healing through my personal growth.

* I learned that there are certain conversations I have with my siblings that affect them in positive or negative ways. I began to be aware and conscious of their triggers and I chose to have conversations that impacted them positivity. For example, I wouldn't talk about my success in front of my brother because it brought out his insecurities. I could see his insecurity (life work), but out of respect I wouldn't talk about certain subjects that would really upset him. I would let him know that I was here to talk to him about anything and that my door is always open.

* I began to give love and let go of the opinions that used to bother me. I choose to give attention to the positive (inner superhero style) because focusing on positive brings in more positive.

* My own healing facilitated growth which allowed me to get to know my family members on a deeper level - I did my growth challenges with them around. For example, I engaged in the three-day silence exercise with them!

Celebrate a positive in the past!

Think of activities that you did when you were a child that brought you so much fun and happiness. Think about music, playground games, movies, card games, spending time with a family member or friend, etc. Whatever it is, I want you to write down three activities that bring you or brought you happiness! Get ready Go!

Happiness is the way.

1.

____

____

____

____

2.

____

____

____

____

3.

____

____

____

____

Erica's Examples:

1. Spending time with my brother watching Disney movies! We loved *The Lion King*.
2. Having a mom and daughter night!
3. Track and Field meets. I loved fitness!

"SUPERHERO FRIENDSHIPS HERE WE COME"

HOW I CREATED SUPERHERO FRIENDSHIPS

Friendships - How to Create Superstar Friendships!

This is one of my favourite sections because I think there is a BIG opportunity for students to come together and support one another. There is too much bullying out there among students. Some students feel the need to put others down because they don't feel good about themselves. We need to stop this today by being and leading with love, healthy self esteem, and confidence with one another.

I had to break up with some friends who were not moving with me on my life journey.

When I moved to the group home I didn't know anyone. I was turning over a new leaf by going to rehab and I knew that I had to attract new healthy friends. I had to let go of the friends who were getting into trouble. I was scared because I thought I might be alone and that no one would like me because of my past - going to juvi, drugs, drinking, etc. But something inside me had faith and I did the best I could to live life to find new friends. There were times when I felt like a loner **(even superheroes fly SOLO missions!)**, but I knew that by sticking to my plan at some point I would meet new people! After all, I was searching to find myself. I had just gone through intense healing activities in rehab as well as a move to a new city. I had to be patient with me and life on life's terms. With the advice of the group home staff and my desire to make new friends, I started taking action! I took fitness classes, got a job, and created a social justice and peace group at school. I met some amazing people who were happy and treated me with love and respect. Their happiness rubbed off on me! It was through taking action that I was able to make new awesome healthy friends! I felt so happy, secure, and thankful for my new life and clean slate!

I use the following techniques to build friendships.

* I don't talk negatively about people and I don't talk behind people's backs. These behaviours do not align with your inner superhero and negatively impact your self esteem. (If you talk behind someone's back to someone else, that person will clearly talk behind anyone else's back too).

* I lead by example: I offer compliments and do nice things for my friends like sending them loving positive quotes, buying them flowers, cooking dinner together, attending classes together, etc.

* I smile and am friendly with others.

* I attend extracurricular activities to meet new people :) I walk up and introduce myself to someone and ask their name :)

* I look for qualities in people that I LOVE and am not afraid to ask them to hang out.

I am so happy and grateful to be sharing these stories with you!

Now, I want you to think about building your superhero friendships. Think of it like the Avengers who work together as a team for a common goal. They celebrate and embrace each other's unique superpowers.

Super Sisters' or Super Brothers' Friendships!

When friends bring out each other's inner superheroes by celebrating each other superpowers and leading by example when the inner villain comes out, relationships can strengthen and develop!

Write down reasons WHY it is so important to be superheroes with your friends and WHY it is important to bring out the inner superheroes within others.

____

____

____

____

Who are your Superhero Friends?

Write their names down here and list three qualities that you LOVE about them. Explain why you enjoy them being in your life.

____

____

____

____

Write down three activities that you want to do or already enjoy doing with your friends.

____

____

____

____

If you want to build new friendships, how can you do that? Write down activities you can participate in to meet new people.

____

____

____

____

Write down HOW you can build relationships with these people.

____

____

____

____

Gratitude Card/Video Challenge

Pick 12 people in your life who you LOVE. You are going to create a handwritten card or send a video to them telling them WHY you LOVE having them in your life. Express why you appreciate them. Speak from the heart. What is meant to come out will come out.

Learning how to build and let go of friendships is a life skill that will serve you well, not just in the school years but in life. Friendships are important to feel important, happy, and special in life. I love my friends and have so much fun with them! They celebrate life milestones, have my back during challenging times, and create lasting fun memories together all while living life and trying new experiences like food, travel, fitness, and more!

You deserve to have the best, loving, healthy, happy friends!

YOU DESERVE LOVE,
HEALTH & HAPPINESS!

Dating Relationships

Dating and engaging in a boyfriend and girlfriend relationship is part of growing up. This relationship is important because this person is your best friend, accountability partner, and VIP - Very Important Peep. J For most of us, it takes many dating relationships to find the one to spend the rest of our life with. My goal with this section is to share stories of my dating relationships to empower students to make healthy and happy decisions when it comes to dating. It's important to make these decisions and pick the best person suitable for who you are and your life goals. For example, pick someone who uplifts you and brings out the best within you (your inner superhero).

* Please speak to someone you trust if you have any questions or are going through a difficult time with relationships.

Know your Self Worth!

I would like to spend some time here on revealing my dating history growing up. Knowing your own self worth helps you to establish your own standards and expectations. Often, we get stuck in repeating a cycle of our parents' relationships and sometimes we get stuck with adopting unhealthy relationship behaviours. This was true for me when I started dating. There are many types and forms of unhealthy relationships. I believe that the key to unlocking the relationship of your dreams is to establish your self-worth, self esteem, and confidence. What will you settle for, and what won't you settle for? My idea of a successful, healthy, vibrant, and full of love relationship is seeing a relationship as an addition to your already complete, awesome, independent, and wholesome person. The goal here is two independent beings coming together as a whole to form a place where you can be your complete self with, overcome challenges with, and achieve life goals independently and together.

"We get in life what we feel we are worth."

I've seen too many people settle in relationships. As a child I witnessed people being in relationships because of money or out of loneliness. In my opinion, this isn't success. When it is time for dating, you deserve to pick who you want; you deserve to be treated with respect, honour, and love. You are worthy of a healthy, honest, and happy relationship.

Don't settle in life!

Think about it: this is the person with whom you will create a life together - if you choose. There is no more important relationship than this in life except yours.

Let's look at the stats. How many relationships end in domestic abuse? How many relationships end in separation or divorce? Too many. These types of relationships impact the lives of children and often in negative ways.

My relationship pattern

As I mentioned, in the beginning years of dating I selected people who mirrored a similar relationship as my parents' relationship. These relationships were characterized by insecurity, jealousy, co-dependency, lack of communication, lack of respect, abuse, etc. Put simply, I didn't know what a healthy relationship was. It was going through a bad breakup that involved the cops, loss of my job, which almost led me to living in a women's shelter. When I woke up my inner superhero I began to attract different people and learned qualities of a healthy relationship that has brought me so much happiness today.

Throughout the school years, I didn't think I was worthy of a handsome, kind guy. I didn't know what a healthy relationship was. I was in relationships that were abusive. I adopted my relationship to my identity. I would agree with everything my boyfriend felt, and I would engage in all the activities and sports that he was interested in. I would cancel hanging out with family and friends. I also remember wanting to get pregnant from a boyfriend because he was moving, and I thought if I got pregnant from him then I could keep him.

There was a period of time that I "dated" myself!

When I woke up my inner superhero I finally started to see the abusive patterns I had adopted in my life. I started to see that I settled for relationships out of fear of being alone. I realized I was scared of being alone, and I didn't think of my own needs, identity, goals, and passions. I was repeating behaviour I had learned from my parents that was not my greatness or inner superhero. I noticed that my thoughts were aligned with focusing on getting married and having kids; however, I realized that I had other life goals that I wanted to accomplish first. After my awakening I became aware.

So I took a time out and began to "date" Erica. I knew I needed to get to know me before I could date someone else. I wanted to get to know who I was and strengthen the relationship I had with myself. I didn't realize how dating Erica would be so much fun! I would cook nice dinners for me, go for walks, buy myself a gift, etc. Using this process I was developing a strong sense of self through giving time to me through personal care and personal growth activities. I was strengthening my self esteem, confidence, and personal power. I developed wicked amounts of self love activities that paid dividends! This process took about one year. When I was ready to date again, I began to attract different types of guys (law of attraction). I attracted gentlemen through creating my own dating standards. This was so empowering and exciting for me. I realized that I had the power to create healthy relationships and could have set myself up for success in the dating world all along. I just hadn't know this back in my early dating years.

What is a healthy relationship?

A healthy relationship exists when there is a connection based on mutual respect, trust, honesty, and good communication while maintaining your own identity. An unhealthy relationship exists when those ingredients are lost. When people feel disrespected and lied to and there are unbalanced communication levels, etc. then they are in an unhealthy relationship. There are many forms of healthy and unhealthy relationships.

Every girl deserves to be treated like a princess, and every boy deserves to be treated like a prince!

Note: I don't believe in a fantasy world of "perfect" relationships like we see through Disney. But I do believe that it is possible to build, create, and grow the relationship of your dreams! I believe it takes a wicked strong relationship with self; high levels of self esteem, confidence, and personal, communication; and recognizing your partner's inner superhero and their life mission.

Let's establish some healing ground rules and standards for dating relationships.

Erica's Example

I choose to only be in healthy relationships where I get to choose my friends.

I choose to be in healthy relationships where I have a voice and will be heard.

I choose to be in relationships where we each have our own activities and interests.

I choose to be in relationships where I am treated with love and respect.

I choose to be in relationships where I can personally and professionally grow with my partner.

I choose to be in relationships where my partner wants to volunteer with me and help out in the community.

I choose to be in relationships where my partner and I share common goals, and where I can attend some of his activities and interests.

I choose to be in relationships with mutual respect.

YOUR TURN!

You may already be dating or will be in the future. Regardless, I want you to think about healthy behaviours, boundaries, and expectations.

I choose to be in a relationship that involves:

____

____

____

____

____

____

____

____

* Dating relationships are designed to enhance your happiness, like a best friend who empowers you to achieve goals and dreams and overcome personal roadblocks that prevent success. Please be conscious of your choices and decision making as you grow through the student years.

EMPOWERING OTHER EMPOWERS YOU!

Empower Yourself through Empowering Others!

Mother Teresa said "some people come in your life as blessings and some come in your life as life lessons."

I began serving others when I moved to the group home. When I decided to get involved, I wanted to give back to the community for what I had taken away, to build new friendships, and to be a part of something.

Serving others through volunteering in women's shelters and raising funds for kids in Haiti allowed me to see that I was not alone. I learned that there are other people going through challenges on the planet. Volunteering humbled me. Volunteering showed me that I am not the only person on the planet. It gave me a sense of connection and community and I saw that I was not alone with internal suffering and goals in life.

When we serve others we are serving ourselves!

It felt so good to work with others through volunteering. Through servicing others, I realized that I was doing good for me. I volunteered to provide services or raise funds to provide the basic necessities of life, and I was so happy to provide for others.

I was served as well.

I am ever so grateful to live in Canada and to be provided the opportunity to live in the group home. Through living in the group home I learned basic life skills. The group home provided me with the opportunity to go to rehab, and they set me up to live on my own in a healthy environment. One thing I've learned in life is that the challenges we go through are actually opportunities to grow as a human being. When we grow through opportunities we can truly relate with others who are suffering, who are lost, and who need guidance. We can use our own setbacks to set up for others' success. This is why I have dedicated my entire life to serving others through sharing my story and teachings. I want to give others the tools to help themselves.

What I learned from serving others

We often find ourselves in the service of others.

We can learn from everyone who enters into our lives.

Spending time with people can be one of the biggest gifts to offer someone on this planet. It is a language of love. This is a love so proud that it cannot be replaced by anything else.

How are you currently involved in your community? What have you thought about doing?

____

____

____

____

How can you become involved in your community? What resources can you tap into to find ways to get involved in activities you enjoy? How can you create a win-win situation for you, the volunteer placement, and the people involved?

____

____

____

____

Community Activity

Research some places in your community that need volunteers. Focus on finding places that connect with some of your hobbies and interests. Ask your neighbours and friends if they have any recommendations. Schedule a day to go learn about a volunteer opportunity.

Notes:

ARE YOU LISTENING TO YOUR INNER SUPERHERO?

DO YOU KNOW
THE TWO MOST
IMPORTANT DAYS
OF YOUR LIFE?

The Two Most Important Days of Your Life are the day you are born and the day you realize why you are born. BAM!

When I think about life I often think about people's life's purpose. I can't think of a more important goal than to realize your very own life's purpose. Finding your life's purpose is so important because it brings inner joy; it is the reason that you are born!

Your life's purpose is WHY you are here. Some call this your true calling. I believe that every human being is born for a reason. Our birthday is the first most important day! The day that we realize WHY we are born is the second most important day. Everyone has a life's purpose. Your life's purpose can be many things and your life's purpose can fluctuate through the days, especially as we grow through the different stages in life.

Your Life's Purpose is Your MAIN SUPERHERO MISSION

If you haven't noticed yet, I love to lead by example, which is why I have written my own answers down in the sections where I ask you questions. I wouldn't ask you to do something I haven't tried and haven't seen succeed :)

Erica's Main Superhero Mission

Through awakening my inner superhero, I realized that everyone has a life purpose. I remember the day I realized mine. I was running outside along a route that I often ran and it just hit me. My life's purpose is simple: to inspire, educate, and empower others to discover and live their life on purpose while discovering their life's purpose. My life's purpose varies in different forms based on the types of relationships that I have in my life. For example, on some days my life's purpose is to be an amazing sister, daughter, friend, speaker, coach, etc. My life's purpose is ever evolving and shifting. For example, the purpose of this book is to save souls from negative thinking, bullying, and peer pressure that sometimes results in suicide. The purpose of this book is to teach students of life how to release negative emotions like depression, anxiety, and loneliness through building the qualities of self esteem, confidence, and love by awakening their inner superhero.

Discovering your life's purpose takes time and everyone has their own timing. Some people know sooner than others. That is okay. Trust the timing. It's important to not compare to others but to relate. Everyone's life purpose is different. In the meantime, it doesn't hurt to start thinking about your life's purpose. What do you think your life's purpose is?

What is your true calling, life purpose, or main superhero mission?

By engaging and following through with all the building blocks to connect and awaken your inner superhero you will find your life's purpose. Follow along in the next section that discusses goals and dreams. Trust that the realization will come to you at the right time! Please feel free to share with me your life's purpose by contacting me through my website! I would LOVE to hear it! www.ericahumphrey.com

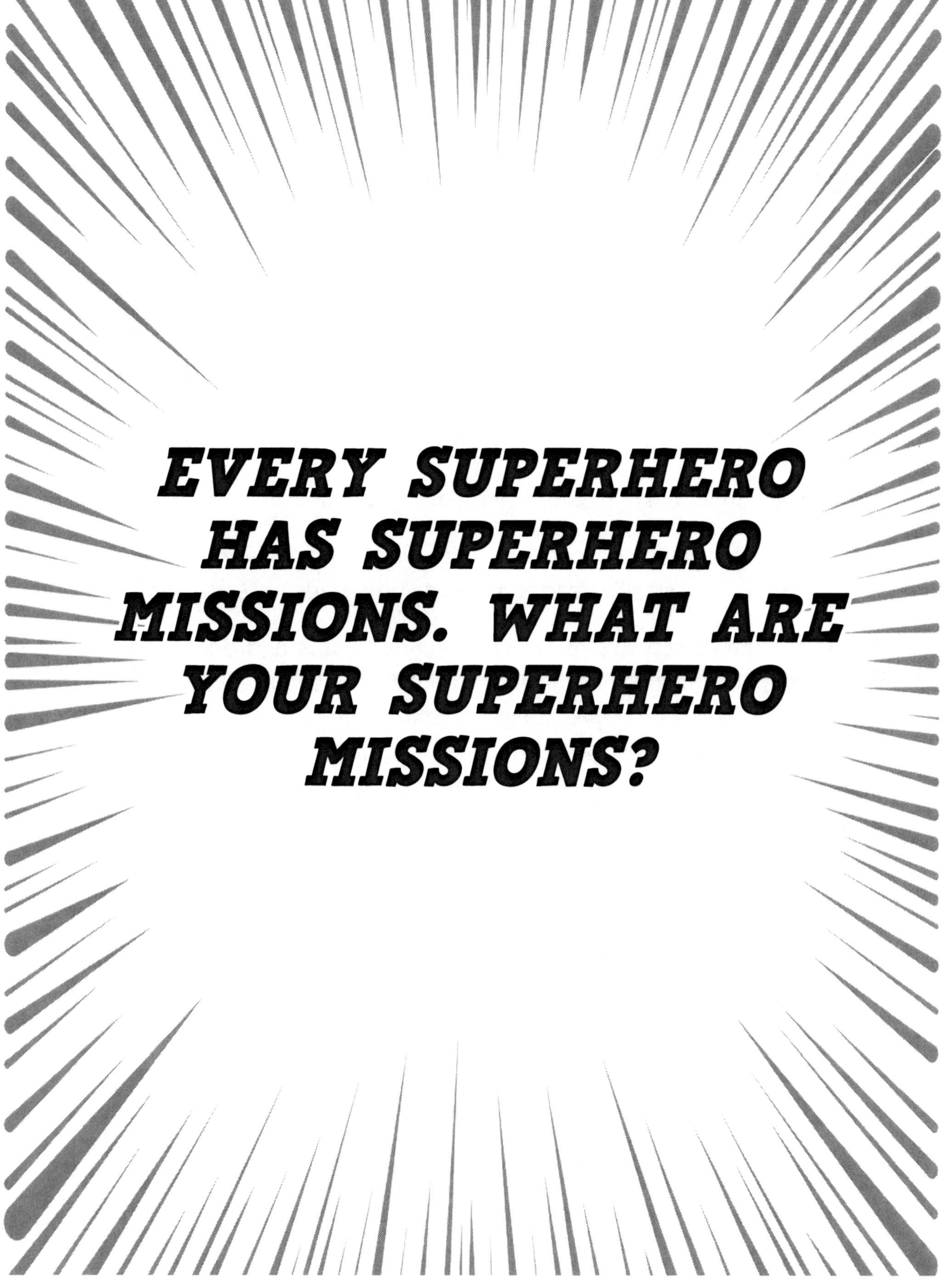
EVERY SUPERHERO HAS SUPERHERO MISSIONS. WHAT ARE YOUR SUPERHERO MISSIONS?

What are your superhero missions?

Congratulations! You have now completed the three building blocks. These building blocks will set you up for the highest success rate in achieving your goals and dreams!

It takes many ingredients to bring a dream to life and create success. I want to be real with you by letting you know that some goals will be easier than others. I have created this workbook to set you up for success. Apply the work from the previous chapters to aid you in achieving your superhero missions, a.k.a. your goals and dreams!

Note: Your superhero missions are your goals and dreams :)

Doing the previous workbook building blocks will increase the achievement success rate of your goals and dreams!

I am so excited for you to embark on your goals and dreams, a.k.a. your superhero missions. I promise it is so rewarding and worthy of doing the life work to get here. It takes building your foundation; learning the power of thoughts and intention; focusing on how to clear up your past baggage of fears, disappointments, and hurts; and building relationships and recognizing who you are - your natural born talents, gifts, abilities, and skills (superpowers) to enhance your success rate in achieving your life goals and dreams! When you continue to engage in your life work, you will experience personal growth and develop mentally, emotionally, physically, and spiritually. You will be strong, powerful, and fearless to go after your goals and dreams! NOW, let's talk about what they are!

What are your goals and dreams?

So I ask you: what are your goals and dreams? What do you daydream about? If you could do or be anything on this planet, what would that be, and what would that look like? What is your vision for your life?

When we think about our goals and dreams in life, we often think about the job or career we want to have. While this is important, there are other factors that are tied into our individual life goals and dreams. Other factors are tied into your dream job. For example, goals do not just exist around work, but around building relationships, friendships, physical health, mental health, life experiences, and more.

ANYTHING IS POSSIBLE - DREAM UP THE POSSIBILITIES

Whether you are looking to achieve great grades in school; earn a scholarship; overcome negative thinking, bullying, peer pressure, or influence; lose weight; build a healthy body image; overcome an addiction; enhance your confidence at work or self esteem for your relationships; make new friends, etc. - there are clear processes and mindset patterns to engage in daily that will create the achievement of your desired outcomes.

I want you to start thinking. I want you to get the creative mental juices flowing to think about what you want out of life.

Some Questions to Think About

Where are you at in your life? Where are you heading? What are your current life goals and dreams? What is holding you back from achieving your goals? Where are the opportunities to turn a setback into a set up for success?

Life Coaching Questions

Here are some life coaching questions to get you thinking before your brainstorming session.

As a Life Coach, I teach, inspire, and educate others to focus on life goals and dreams. Here are some questions that I use in my sessions for others to create their own superhero success stories! Take a look!

Let's Brainstorm

One of the activities in this section that we are going to do together will be a brainstorming session of ideas. We will do this without having any attachment to the outcome, because without attachment you will release more information. The focus here is to get as many ideas on paper as possible, to get in a rhythm and flow, to allow your creativity to unfold, and to express your inner superhero wisdom. The ultimate mission here is to create a balanced healthy lifestyle fueled with passion, health, and happiness.

Next, we are going to brainstorm and build upon your previous work. The goal is to write out your heart's desire of your goals and dreams. Remember we are brainstorming with no attachment - just keep writing things down. Take as long as you want. There is no time limit.

READY, ON YOUR MARK, GET SET, GO!!!!

Superhero Style Brainstorming Exercise

Write down your goals and dreams!

Erica's Goals and Dreams!

Great JOB! How did that feel? I LOVE this exercise because it is so much fun for me and never gets old! You can do this exercise with anyone, anytime.

Erica's Goals and Dreams

Allow me to share some of my past and present goals and dreams. In the past, I wanted to overcome suicidal and negative thinking and depression. I wanted to enhance my self esteem and self love and to achieve business and life goals. It was through awakening my inner superhero and acknowledging my superhero superpowers that I was able to attain my goals and dreams.

Erica's Past Goals and Accomplishments

* Attend Post Secondary Education. I was and still am the only person in my family who has attended college.

* Travel the world. I have travelled to Bali, Indonesia; Seoul, South Korea; Paris, France; London, England; Mexico; Dominican Republic; Miami, Florida; Dallas, Texas; San Diego, California; and the East Coast of Canada.

* Win Instructor of the Year - Fitness Franchisee Model Company

* Learn how to overcome negative thinking, depression, and anxiety.

* Create a business that I am madly in love with to live my life on purpose.

* Develop entrepreneurship skills. I ran my first business when I was 19.

Erica's Present Goals

* To build a strong network of like-minded people

* To build group homes and shelters while investing in life education in these homes to promote growth, health, and happiness

* Travel to Spain, Italy, Switzerland, and the West Coast of Canada

* Go on a mom and daughter Caribbean trip

* Create a power couple style relationship

Activities to Achieve your Goals and Dreams!

Now that you have written out some of your goals and dreams, what can you do with these ideas? I am sharing with you some activities I engage in and LOVE to draw out more of my goals and dreams.

Google Your Dreams!

I love finding inspiration through living life because what I discover is an extension of my inner superhero. Once I write my goals and dreams down, I like to Google the items and see what I find. For example, when I was planning a trip to Miami and Cali, I loved to Google what those places looked like. I loved to read articles on awesome adventures and activities to engage in, local restaurants to eat at, and any other recommendations I could find.

Make a Vision and Dream Board for Fun!

I love creating vision and dream boards because they are so much fun. It is cool to see the pictures of my dreams. Vision boards guide me to visualize my dreams and put them in my mind. I've made vision boards by myself and with others. I use newspapers, magazines, and print materials to make a beautiful vision board. To view some of my vision boards go to: www.ericahumphrey.com.

Ask others what their goals and dreams are!

I love asking other people what their goals and dreams are because it is exciting to talk about them about their passions. I find that most people are excited to share as well. Focus on the people who want to have these conversations; you may be surprised where the conversation takes you. Remember, what we put out in the world comes back to us.

Painting Pictures

I love being creative and releasing my thoughts and emotions through painting. I also love to draw, colour, and scrapbook! It feels good to create beautiful pictures of my passions and loves in life. What activities do you like to engage in that bring you joy?

Calendar

Schedule the activities that you need to do to get closer to achieving your goals and dreams. Find a system that works best for you. The best system is the one you use!

Know your priorities and stick to them!

When determining HOW to achieve a goal I highly recommend to outline your top priorities in life to make decisions. Remember, what you spend most of your time doing you will become. Sometimes in life we need to make short term sacrifices to achieve the results we are looking in the long term.

Learn from people who are a few steps ahead of you!

When I put my thinking cap on to achieve and goal, I turn to people who have achieved what I want and ask them how they did it! Use your superpowers, your strength and passion to go after what you want. Mirror similar success to achieve yours.

Use meditation and physical fitness activities to enhance your focus to build your productivity level. When you are focusing on how to achieve a goal, focus on being present in the moment to get more work done.

Failure is your learning lessons!

Use failure as feedback for your personal growth to achieve your goals and dreams. Choose to use failure or any set backs are motivation to continue on your journey. It is just going to make it sweeter when you hit your goal!

BELIEVE IN YOURSELF THAT YOU CAN DO IT! LEARN FROM YOUR MISTAKES AND KEEP MOVING FORWARD UNTIL YOU ACHIEVE THE GOAL YOU DESIRE. REMEMBER LIFE ISN'T PERFECT SO YOU DON'T HAVE TO BE!

Surround yourself around great people!
Greatness attracts greatness!

Next, I am going to share some life coaching questions I use with clients. ENJOY!

SUPERHERO SUCCESS QUESTIONS

Self Esteem + Confidence + Personal Power = Success Stories

If you have a genie to ask for 3 wishes what would your three wishes be?

____

____

____

____

What would you do if you knew you wouldn't fail?

____

____

____

____

What would get you out of bed every morning early and fuel you to get to work and school?

____

____

____

____

What does success look like for you?

____

____

____

____

What places do you want to travel to?

____

____

____

____

What is something you have always wanted to do but haven't done yet? Why haven't you done it yet?

____

____

____

____

Who are the coaches, mentors, and teachers in your life that can positively affect you? I like to find several people who have different strengths that I can learn from!

Notes:

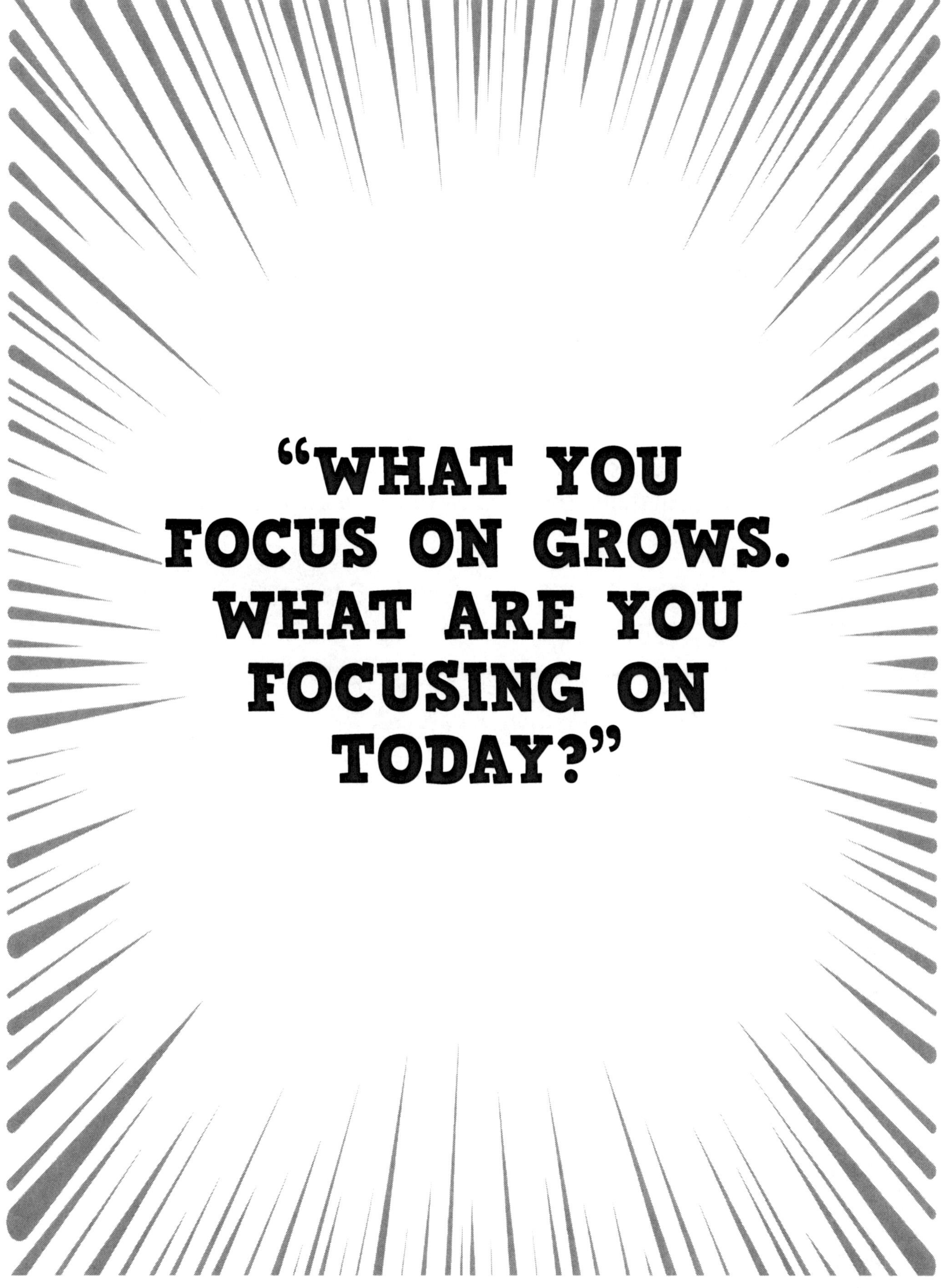
"WHAT YOU FOCUS ON GROWS. WHAT ARE YOU FOCUSING ON TODAY?"

Affirmations

READ THE AFFIRMATIONS BELOW FROM "I CAN DO IT" CALENDAR THAT A FRIEND BOUGHT ME WHICH I LOVE!!!

Incorporating affirmations into my daily routine has been and still is a life changer for me and others. I challenge you to write out and read affirmations that are aligned with your personal goals and dreams.

Allow the affirmations below to inspire you. I want you to think about your goals and dreams and create a few affirmations on your own. Before you write out some of your own, I want to share some of MY FAVOURITE affirmations that I have found to be powerful in my life.

"Love is the nourishment that as humans we need to fulfill our greatness. As I learn to love myself more, I learn to love everyone more. Together we tenderly cultivate an ever more beautiful world."

"I treat each person I encounter during the day with kindness. I receive that same consideration in return."

"I am filled with boundless energy. I awaken each morning eager for the new experiences to come."

"I love and approve of myself and I easily choose thoughts that thrill me."

"I am thankful for my wonderful life. I accept with joy and pleasure and gratitude all the good universe offers me."

"Today I remind myself that I can make the choice to feel good."

"I am constantly discovering new ways to improve my health."

"Long lasting loving relationships brighten my life."

"It is easy for me to get centred. Even in the midst of stress, I can relax."

"As I begin a new day, I let go of the past and become a "now" person. This month marks a fresh start for me, and I welcome it with open arms."

"Working together is part of the purpose of life. I am learning about love at my job. I love the people I work with."

"I have the divine right to be fulfilled in all avenues of life. I am worthy of success."

"Life brings me only good experiences. I am open to new and wonderful changes."

"My home is such a happy place to be! I bless everyone who enters, myself included. Pleasant experiences fill every room."

"Compliments are gifts of prosperity. I have learned to accept them graciously."

"Being around my pets and feeling their unconditional love makes me feel so good."

"I now move into a new era of prosperity and abundance. Thank you LIFE!"

"When it is time for a new job, the perfect position presents itself easily."

"I easily fit into every area of life. I am an excellent communicator in all situations."

"All that I need to know at any given moment is revealed to me. My intuition is always on my side."

"My job allows me to express my talents and abilities, and I am grateful for this employment."

"I have the power to change my life for the better, and I am doing so now."

"Today I fulfill my creative side. I know I can bloom wherever I am planted."

"I have a special guardian angel. I am divinely guided and protected at all times."

"Divine right action is guiding me every moment of the day."

"This is an excellent day to clear clutter and complete old projects."

"Forgiving makes me feel free and light. I forgive everyone, including myself."

"Opportunities are everywhere. I have a multitude of choices."

"I now give myself the green light to go ahead, and to joyously embrace the new."

"Whenever I travel, I am protected and safe. I always have an enjoyable time."

"I am unlimited in my wealth. All areas of my life are abundant and fulfilling."

"What I concentrate on is exactly what I will attract. Joy brings joy."

"I am a bright, capable person. With my thoughts, I can create an ever more rewarding life."

"Yesterday is done and gone. Today is the first day of my future."

"I view all experiences as opportunities for me to learn and grow."

"I know that all is well, and even better things are coming to me."

"I give to others all the things I want to receive. In this way, we bless and prosper each other."

"Today I choose to see my life as an adventure. I uproot outdated beliefs and discover hidden treasures of joy and freedom."

"Each day I express more fully the inner beauty and strength of my true being."

"I do something new – or at least different – every day."

"I am part of the Universe; therefore, I know that there is an order, rhythm, and purpose to my life."

"I am grateful for Life's generosity. I am so blessed."

"I get plenty of sleep every night. My body appreciates how I take care of it."

Write out affirmations for your life goals and dreams!

____

____

____

____

To take this step further, place these affirmations in your phone, on your mirror, on your Facebook wall, etc. Put these powerful affirmations in places where you look often so that you can program your mind to build and strengthen your mental muscles for success, health, and happiness in your life.

Now, are you ready? It is time to unleash your inner superhero by engaging in the following exercise. This is your life! This is your time! The time is now! Go for it and remember that you have this inner superhero to use anytime you want in your life! I can't wait to hear your story!

BUILD YOUR OWN SUPERHERO

Erica's Inner Superhero

Superhero Name: Erica Effect

Superhero Powers: Positivity, Passion for Fitness, Empowering others, Making things Happen, Courage, Listening to others.

Superhero Mission: To teach students how to awaken their inner superhero, identify their super powers to overcome school challenges, and achieve their dreams by building self esteem, confidence, personal power, and resilient muscles.

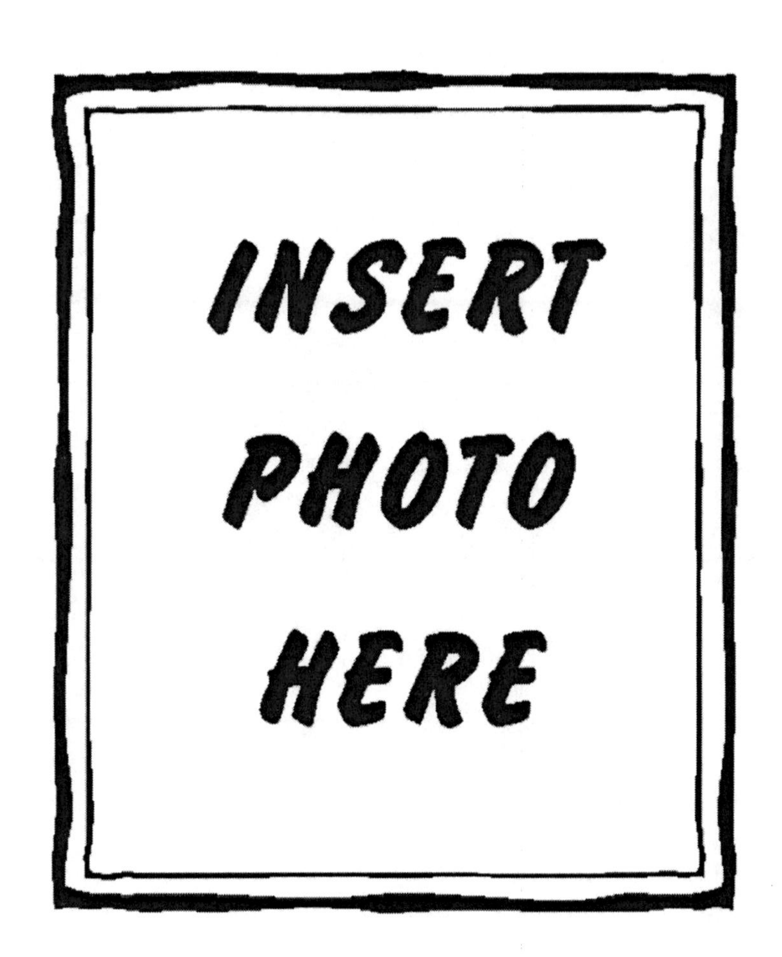

Your Inner Superhero

What is your Superhero Name?

What are your Superhero Powers?

What are your Superhero Missions?

Writing Your Superhero Pledge

Your superhero pledge is your code to live by. This pledge that you create will be a guideline on how you want to live your life. Think of what you would love to see in a superhero. Write the qualities that you LOVE to see in you. Write out your core values, mission, vision, whatever message is important for you to read often. Take a look at mine as an example.

ERICA'S SUPERHERO PLEDGE

I pledge to empower, inspire, and uplift students to break through school challenges. By passionately offering life education through speaking events, engaging activities, sharing stories, and encouraging life building challenges, students learn how to add tools to their tool belt and hit challenges head-on.

I want every student to feel good about who they are by being able to look themselves in the mirror and feel comfortable in their own skin. Every student should know that they are worthy of love, health, happiness, and success.

Inspired through the process of awakening my own inner superhero, I feel motivated to show students how to overcome negative thoughts, bullying, and peer pressure through achieving personal goal and dreams, all while discovering who they are.

I dream of a world where students do not hold themselves back from seizing opportunities for any reason at all. I dream of a world where students feel empowered to take action towards building a healthy lifestyle.

I dream of a world where students feel safe to be their true authentic self through taking action to ignite their "superpowers" (unique gifts, talents, abilities, and skills) and to realize their own personal power to be resilient, confident, and strong as they rise above any challenge and achieve any dream.

This book is created to give you action steps, formulas, games, and life challenges to awaken your inner superhero! By the end of this book, you will build and celebrate your own inner superhero.

I know that anything is possible. I commit to being a fearless leader who inspires change and leads by example by growing personally and professionally.

I promise to take care of me! I promise to take care of my physical, emotional, mental, spiritual, and relational health because I deserve love, health, happiness, and a clean slate!

I promise to give back to my community and serve others because I know when I participate in life events and give back I am giving to myself and putting karma in the bank.

Life is about relationships, and I know that the more people I serve, the healthier and happier I am.

I pledge to think highly of myself and treat myself with love, honour, and respect. When I am feeling upset or emotional, I promise to do the best I can to release my emotions in a healthy way. I ask for help when needed. I choose not to gossip.

My Superhero Pledge

Erica's Top 10 Favourite Books

1. *How to Think and Grow Rich*
2. *21 Irrefutable Laws of Leadership*
3. *5 Languages of Love*
4. *The Power of Now*
5. *10 Stupid Things Women do to Mess Up Their Lives*
6. *Heal Your Life*
7. *The Power of Intention*
8. *Your Sacred Self*
9. *The Power of your Subconscious Mind*
10. *All is well*

Resources

1. Kids Help Phone
2. Big Brothers and Big Sisters Organization
3. http://teenmentalhealth.org/
4. http://www.mentalhealthhelpline.ca/

JOIN THE I AM MY OWN SUPERHERO FACEBOOK GROUP

Designed to be a respectful, safe, cool, non-judgmental zone to honour and celebrate your inner superhero.

Join the group and share your inner superhero creation.

This is a forum for like-minded individuals to share successes and ask questions to live an awesome and cool life!

Connect with Erica

Website

www.ericahumphrey.com

Facebook

https://www.facebook.com/erica.humphrey.33

LinkedIn

https://www.linkedin.com/in/erica-humphrey-5662b326

Twitter

https://twitter.com/ericaeffect12

Instagram

https://www.instagram.com/ericaeffect12/

Blog

http://www.ericahumphrey.com/news/

Bring Erica to Speak

To schedule Erica for a speaking event,
workshop, or fitness class contact:

Enhance Performance

Cambridge, Ontario

1-844-4BE-HERO

Visit Erica on the Internet

www.ericahumphrey.com

So my question to you is, what are you waiting for? I dare you right now to take actions towards setting yourself up for success in school and life. Stop waiting for something to change or appear in your life. Stand up and be your own superhero!

To Be Continued...

CPSIA information can be obtained
at www.ICGtesting.com
Printed in the USA
LVOW09s1501291216
519136LV00002B/45/P

9 781524 610890